THINK
TO WIN

THINK TO WIN

THE STRATEGIC DIMENSION
OF TENNIS

ALLEN FOX

HarperPerennial
A Division of HarperCollins Publishers
An Edward Burlingame Book

THINK TO WIN: THE STRATEGIC DIMENSION OF TENNIS. Copyright © 1993 by Allen Fox. All rights reserved. Printed in the United States of America. No part of this book may be used or reproduced in any manner whatsoever without written permission except in the case of brief quotations embodied in critical articles and reviews. For information address HarperCollins Publishers, Inc., 10 East 53rd Street, New York, NY 10022.

HarperCollins books may be purchased for educational, business, or sales promotional use. For information please write: Special Markets Department, HarperCollins Publishers, Inc., 10 East 53rd Street, New York, NY 10022.

FIRST EDITION

Designed by Ruth Kolbert

Library of Congress Cataloging-in-Publication Data

Fox, Allen.
    Think to win : the strategic dimension of tennis / Allen Fox.
        p.   cm.
    Includes index.
    ISBN 0–06–098200–4 (pbk.)
    1. Tennis—Psychological aspects.   I. Title.
GV1002.9.P75F696   1993
796.342′01′9—dc20   92–53397

93 94 95 96 97 AC/CW 10 9 8 7 6 5 4 3 2 1

To Nancy, Evan, and Charlie

This Book Was Written in Collaboration with Michael Fox

Michael Fox was instrumental in the creation of this book. Michael's thoughts helped guide the conceptual process every step of the way. He reviewed, corrected, and added ideas to every chapter of this book. His brilliant insights into the subtle points of strategy and the mechanics of the strokes have been essential ingredients in making this book different from most tennis books.

Michael Fox resides in Toowoomba, Australia, with his wife, Karen, and his children, Cara and Jeremy. He is a renowned tennis coach and analyst. He writes a monthly article for *Tennis Magazine,* Australia, on the mental aspects of tennis. Michael also counsels and guides the careers of some of Australia's top tennis players and Olympic athletes.

Acknowledgment to Norman Zeitchick

One my greatest pleasures in writing *Think to Win* has been observing Norman Zeitchick's brilliant editorial mind at work. His years as a senior editor at *Tennis Magazine* have given him a wealth of tennis knowledge and the ability to transmit complex ideas in a clear and simple manner. He has turned my sentences and paragraphs around so that the flow of information is natural and easy to read. In fact, after working with Norman for the past year, I have so completely absorbed his style that I can hardly put pen to paper without feeling that he is looking over my shoulder and nudging me to rearrange subject and predicate. I am greatly in Norman's debt for helping me to create this book.

CONTENTS

PREFACE

There are more than 20 million tennis players in the United States and most of them play below their actual capabilities. Why? Because the emphasis in instruction is on how to *hit the ball* better rather than on how to *play* better, and these are two quite different things.

Your ability to play up to your potential involves not only the ability to hit your strokes with control and power, but, even more important, the understanding of how to use these strokes in order to win. This is where strategy comes in, and strategy is what this book is about.

Let me illustrate what I mean. I used to enjoy watching a regularly scheduled match on the Pepperdine University courts between Jim Harrick, the head basketball coach (now at UCLA) and a professor of social science. Some few people, fortunately for them, just seem to be born with an innate sense for strategy, and Jim is such a person. The professor possessed well-manicured strokes, obviously developed under the careful scrutiny of a tennis pro who knew what he was doing. He hit the ball beautifully, often with great power and accuracy. Against most opponents, he held a substantial psychological edge just because he looked so darn good.

Jim, on the other hand, looked horrible. He was self-taught and looked like a basketball player who had recently been given a racket as a gift and was enthusiastically trying it out. Jim's backhand was a poked slice and his forehand a slap shot which he muscled into the court. However, Jim was a good athlete and, as you might imagine from his profession, ferociously competitive. He had a pretty good first serve, fine reflexes, a sturdy pair of legs, and that was about it. But Jim knew how to play.

They fought some epic battles and, much to my surprise, Jim invariably came out on top. This was, at first, incomprehensible. The professor was obviously a trained player and Jim, just as obviously, was not. But as I watched, the mystery gradually resolved itself. Jim knew exactly what he was doing and the professor was just hitting shots. The professor was oblivious to the percentages and invariably whacked balls hard and near the lines. He made lots of mistakes. Jim dinked the ball in the court, ran down enough of the professor's shots to give the professor a chance to miss, and put away enough volleys to keep the professor off balance. Jim understood how to cover up his own weaknesses and take advantage of his opponent's. The professor, meanwhile, relied solely on his strokes. He never had a chance.

Determining an effective strategy requires knowledge and understanding. Strokes, on the other hand, can be rotely learned by simply following the instructions given by a good pro. There are relatively few decisions to be made and you need little understanding. Repetition will usually suffice to hone these motor skills enough to bring your shotmaking up to a reasonable level.

But how to use these skills effectively is more complex. Where should you hit the ball? How hard should you hit it? Under what conditions should you choose one stroke over another? How do you attack your opponent's weaknesses? How do you play percentage tennis? These and a host of similar questions defy short, pat answers. There are simply too many variables for there to be specific instructions on what to do in every situation that could arise on court.

The serious student of the game must, therefore, learn the basic principles of strategy. Only then can he tailor the use of his strokes to react effectively to the multitude of on-court developments. Jim Herrick was lucky. He knew, somehow, instinctively. The rest of us must be taught. This book is designed to give players and coaches at all levels a deeper insight into the fundamentals of the game. Some analysis of stroking techniques is included because, of course, the ability to hit the ball where one wants is certainly of benefit. But in all cases the book aims at increasing the reader's level of *understanding* of what happens on the tennis court. This is not simply another "how-to" manual. It is a "why-to" manual also.

Writing such a book is an ambitious and complex project, but my training and experience have positioned me ideally for the undertaking. I was originally trained as a scientist, having received a B.A. in physics and a Ph.D. in physiological psychology, both from UCLA. And during my lengthy academic training, I played tournament tennis at an international level. I was ranked among the top ten men in the United States five times, a member of the U.S. Davis Cup team three times, and a quarter-finalist at Wimbledon. I experienced enough success to feel comfortable discussing the intricacies of the game at any level.

Despite those achievements, sports did not come easily or naturally to me. I was a better competitor than athlete. The slightest addition to my repertoire of strokes took me endless hours of work on the practice court. I had to break down every element of technique and strategy into its fundamental components so I could plan and consciously direct my work. Fortunately, my scientific training and bent of mind eased the task, as did insights I received from two excellent professionals, Carl Earn and Frank Feltrop.

In the end, reaching a high level of tennis competence was, for me, a triumph of mind over body. Any hope of a tournament victory over the big boys of my day like Arthur Ashe, Roy Emerson, or John Newcombe depended on my making exceptionally efficient use of my limited physical tools. Although I was not good enough to win the Grand

Slam events as they did, I was able to garner my occasional victories by becoming very adept at strategy and very efficient with strokes.

The purpose of this book is to pass this information on to you, so you too can make the best possible use of your physical abilities. There is more attention to the geometry, physics, and logic of the game than is usual in books of this type, but I have deliberately avoided using scientific words whenever possible to make the concepts more easily understood. This is a sophisticated book that appears simple. Underlying everything is an eye toward practicality. In the end it is my intention that by increasing your understanding of how to play, I will help you win more tennis matches yourself or teach others how to win.

ACKNOWLEDGMENTS

First of all, to Nancy Fox, my wonderful wife, who reviewed the manuscripts and supplied encouragement, help, and love throughout the writing process (and everywhere else in my life, for that matter).

To Evan and Charlie Fox, my two beautiful sons, who inspired me to write this book so that they would always have something by which to remember their father.

To Richard Mosk, George Zwerdling, Larry Nagler, Franz Jevne, and Herb Fitzgibbon, my five dearest friends, who took the time to read and make corrections to the manuscript and who have supported me over the years with intelligent advice.

To Charlie Hoeveler, for giving the book its title and helping with my writing style.

To Carl Earn and Frank Feltrop, for teaching me how to play tennis.

To Joel Drucker, Mark Winters, and Ralph Rabago, for reviewing the manuscript and making their substantial stores of tennis knowledge available to me.

To Cynthia Lum, for her beautiful photography.

To Cary Lothringer, for posing for photographs and feeding me balls all afternoon so that I could look good in the pictures.

STRATEGY
AND YOUR STROKES

Tennis strokes are virtually useless without the strategies that give them direction. To explain what I mean, think of your tennis game as a computer system. Tennis strategy plays the same role with tennis strokes as computer software does with computer hardware. And just as the novice computer buff naively assumes that his major expenses are over when he buys an array of fancy mechanical gadgetry, so too does the beginning tennis player look to acquiring proper strokes as the solution to the problem of winning tennis matches. They both eventually discover their error. Computers can do nothing without the software to tell them what to do. By the same token, tennis strokes are equally useless without proper strategies to give them direction.

Strokes and strategies go hand in hand in winning tennis matches. Though most of the strokes and shots that we see today have been around since the dawn of the game, different strokes predominated for periods of time, depending on the prevailing strategies. Let's take a look at the history of men's tennis to get a feel for the interdependent relationship between various strokes and the strategies that drive them.

From the early days of world-class tournament tennis up through World War II, tennis was played primarily from the baseline. Champions like Bill Tilden, Bill Johnston, Rene Lacoste, Henri Cochet, Fred Perry, Don Budge, and Bobby Riggs did come to the net, but generally behind strong ground strokes or after maneuvering their opponents into disadvantageous positions. Players occasionally served and volleyed, but it was only exceptions like Vinnie Richards and Ellsworth Vines who served and volleyed all the time. The prevailing belief, championed vociferously by Bill Tilden, was that the all-out attacking volleyer could never ultimately stand up to the great ground stroker.

In those early days, players usually hit their backhands flat or with backspin, and hit their forehands flat or with light topspin. The players had discovered that these were very efficient ways to hit ground strokes against an opponent on the baseline. You could propel the ball at high velocity without undue effort, and you could regulate depth with great precision. The game was one of defense or maneuvering attack.

All that changed with the emergence of Jack Kramer in the 1940s. He developed fearsome first and second serves which he consistently projected deep in the service box with terrific power. And he invariably came to the net behind them, as well as on all short balls and at every other possible opportunity. In complete opposition to Tilden, Kramer theorized that a baseliner, no matter how good he was, would eventually falter in the face of an unrelenting net attack. And experience proved him right! For the next thirty-five years, the game was dominated by the volleyers.

Kramer is also credited as the originator of the concept of percentage tennis, in which court geometry becomes a primary determinant of shot selection and decisions are kept to a minimum. Kramer's primary objective was to establish an advantageous court position by playing certain shot patterns, regardless of where his opponent was in the court. One of his tenets was that he should almost invariably direct approach shots down-the-line. Kramer was not concerned that his opponent might know in advance where the ball was going. Once he established himself at the net there was little his opponent could do about it anyway.

Kramer had sensed the Achilles' heel of the baseliners of his time. He realized that flat or sliced ground strokes did not make very effective passing shots. A slice in particular will float, and a player who uses slice for a passing shot is extremely vulnerable to an attack at the net. It cannot be hit hard enough to get past a proficient volleyer and still drop down in the court, especially if it is hit crosscourt. Even the flat stroke has limitations in getting over the net and down into the court quickly enough to pass an opponent at acute angles. Another advantage to the net rusher was the fact that most important tournaments were played on fast surfaces with light balls.

Kramer's strategy capitalized on these stroke limitations, and in his wake came a virtual deluge of net rushers. Pancho Gonzales, Frank Sedgeman, Vic Seixas, Lew Hoad, Tony Trabert, Alex Olmedo, Neale Fraser, Mal Anderson, Roy Emerson, Rafael Osuna, and others all found that the baseliners could not stand up to their attack.

In their haste to get to the net at the earliest possible opportunity, some of these great champions neglected to develop fundamentally sound ground strokes. They just didn't spend the time hitting ground strokes. But they were awfully adept at getting to the net. They came in on their own serves all the time, on their opponent's serves whenever they could, and on any short ball. Since the volleyer had the advantage over the baseliner, they responded by not *being* on the baseline! They correctly figured that if they were at the net all the time they would not need to hit many passing shots. And young players wishing to emulate the current Wimbledon or U.S. champions spent their time at the net also, so that the game was eventually dominated by players with unbalanced games—great volleys and mediocre ground strokes.

That situation spawned another evolutionary advance in the game with the emergence of a new group of champions in the 1960s, headed by Rod Laver. Following in the footsteps of his immediate predecessors, Laver became a great volleyer himself and, as they had done, scrambled to the net whenever humanly possible. But Laver also developed a plan B—heavy topspin ground strokes on both his forehand and backhand sides—to pass his fellow volleyers. He found that topspin was effective for passing shots because the ball could be hit extremely hard and still drop down into the court. With heavy topspin, players could hit sharp crosscourt angles which were previously denied to them by the laws of physics. As John Newcombe was later to state, "Topspin has changed the geometry of the court!"

As an interesting aside, Newcombe came after Laver, yet Newcombe had the more antiquated game. He was, of course, a great serve-and-volleyer, but he had a sliced backhand which he could, on occasion, hit flat. This was very much in the mold of the older champions like Pancho Gonzales and Jack Kramer, who had not mastered topspin on the backhand side. Nobody told Laver or Newcombe to use topspin or, for that matter, not to use it. As youngsters they, like most players, simply watched the reigning champions and copied their styles. Laver was just unique in having the insight to figure out that topspin would help his passing shots. Newcombe, as great as he was, did not.

Shortly after Laver, players such as Manuel Santana, Arthur Ashe, and Tom Okker also started using topspin on passing shots, but the game was still basically won at the net. Then, in the mid-1970s, Bjorn Borg ushered in another evolutionary change in tennis strategy. Borg led a group of baseline specialists who hit with very severe, persistent topspin ground strokes and won with defense. They were helped by the introduction of heavy-duty balls and slower courts. But their ability to consistently pass players at the net with heavy topspin effectively killed off the serve-and-volleyers. Baseliners were back in style!

For several years the game was dominated by this group of baseliners. Players like Guillermo Vilas, "Steady" Eddie Dibbs, and Harold Solomon drove opponents crazy with looping, heavy topspin ground strokes which bounced up above shoulder height and made attack very difficult. It was bizarre (not to mention dull) watching Borg and Vilas endlessly trading heavy topspin ground strokes from the baseline. A stroke which had originally evolved because it was good for passing shots had become part of the basic ground stroke repertoire and was being used against other baseliners. Heavy topspin was not designed for baseline exchanges and, in fact, is ill-suited for this purpose.

John McEnroe notwithstanding, in the early 1980s the tournaments were still being won mostly from the baseline by people like Ivan Lendl, Jimmy Connors, Mats Wilander, and a host of tough Swedes. But the game was still evolving. Players were hitting ground strokes flatter and using them more offensively. The game was doubling back on itself—reverting to the styles of Tilden and Budge. In fact, with a great deal of fanfare, Lendl and Wilander even reintroduced the old backhand slice shot. The players could still hit topspin passing shots as well as topspin lobs, so attacking at the net could be done, but only at substantial risk.

By the end of the decade a sprinkling of excellent serve-and-volleyers like Pete Sampras, Boris Becker, and Stefan Edberg had joined McEnroe to dispute the ground strokers for world dominance. But these were volleyers unlike those of old. They had excellent ground strokes and tremendous serves to augment their volleys. These were necessary if they were to stand any chance of overwhelming the awesome ground strokes of their opponents. Using the old technique of chipping and charging to the net against modern players who can hit topspin lobs and passing shots with pinpoint accuracy is like trying to beat up an antagonist's fist with your nose. Under these circumstances the volleyer must come to the net behind serves and approach shots of such severity that the ground stroker does not have the leeway to mount a coordinated defense.

As we've seen, tennis history clearly illustrates the tight interaction between strokes and strategy. No matter what his physical capabilities on court, a player only succeeds if he uses them hand in hand with proper strategies. And each player must eventually develop a clear grasp of what particular strategy allows him to make optimum use of his own physical abilities.

A player who is one-dimensional—who can only do one

thing well on court—may need to stick to one strategy regardless of what style his opponent uses or how well he plays. The strategy that takes advantage of his few strengths is his only chance of winning.

On the other hand, the player who is more versatile and balanced is able to modify his strategy to capitalize on an opponent's weaknesses or protect against an opponent's strengths. The more one-dimensional your game, the less it can be successfully modified during match play.

For example, Alex Olmedo, the 1959 Wimbledon champion, had a great volley, but relatively poor ground strokes. He literally *had* to do or die at the net. If he ran into an opponent whose passing shots were too good, he was just out of luck. In a way that made life comfortingly simple. If Alex got down a set and a service break, he did not have to scratch his head long about whether he should stay back on the baseline and try trading ground strokes. He would have obtained equivalent benefit by jumping in front of a moving bus. His only strategy was to apply constant pressure at the net and assume that somewhere along the line his opponent would crack.

On the other hand, a player like Brad Gilbert, who played for me at Pepperdine University and has been ranked among the world's top ten, can do a little bit of everything. He not only volleys effectively, but hits his ground strokes well and can run all day, so he has a tremendous number of strategic options open. His game has the chameleonlike ability to blend profitably into the situation of the moment, a trait which has been of great help in producing consistent results over the years. He has a different way of beating every opponent on every surface and under every condition of play.

Brad started out as a pure ground stroker, a style at which he was good, but not good enough. So he made it his business to acquire balance. He spent years working on his volley, serve, use of spins, and variations of pace. Lacking the physical capability of being extraordinary at any particular aspect of the game, he has compensated by systematically becoming *pretty* good at almost every aspect. Combined with his brilliant mind for strategy, this has established him among the world's best. And the average player can benefit by taking careful note of the fact that Gilbert's rise in ranking was a direct result of continually adding new tennis weapons, along with the intelligence to use them well.

The lesson to be learned is that balance is the best alternative for the athlete who lacks exceptional physical ability. It's like decathlon athletes. Though known as the world's greatest athletes to the general public, they are thought of by many of their fellow track stars as people who simply lack the ability to be great in any individual event and are forced into the decathlon because it is their only viable alternative. Gilbert has shown there is a parallel in tennis. Most players, however, do not focus on their weaknesses with Gilbert's intensity and technical insight.

Weaknesses can be improved to a greater degree than you might imagine. In fact, the most effective use of practice time is to focus on rectifying weaknesses. The same amount of time devoted to improving strengths will not heighten one's overall standard of play as much. One reason is that a weakness simply has more room for improvement. Strengths are closer to topping out, so it takes a large amount of work to see a small amount of benefit. With the same amount of effort, a weakness can improve a great deal.

But even more important is the fact that improving a weakness opens up additional strategic options. If, for example, you are a baseliner with a weak or nonexistent volley, what will you do if you find yourself being outsteadied by another baseliner? The fact that your opponent may not be able to hit a passing shot to save his life will be of as little value to you as candor to a congressman. A volley is what you need. A more balanced game gives you potential fallback positions when your customary strategy is not working.

In summary, you can achieve a surprisingly large improvement in your tennis performance by expanding your understanding of strategy and remedying your stroke weaknesses—even if only to a small extent—so as to open up more opportunities to use this understanding.

STRATEGY

2

The player without a strategy on the tennis court is like a ship without a rudder. It can still move, but it will take dumb luck to get where it wants to go. The smart tennis player has an overall plan for how he is going to win points. And this plan starts with the understanding that there are only two ways to win points—either you must hit a winner, or your opponent must make an error. Then you increase your chances to win by playing the percentages, maximizing your strengths, exploiting your opponent's weaknesses, and using the very nature of the game to your advantage.

In the broadest sense, all tennis strategy can be boiled down to just two basic categories: offense and defense. Of course, no player can be categorized as totally offensive or totally defensive, but one strategy or the other will usually predominate. Which strategy is best for you depends on your personality, your skills on the court, and your athleticism. The greatest players in the game have included both defensive and offensive specialists. Examples of players who rely or relied primarily on defense are Bjorn Borg, Chris Evert, Tracy Austin, Mats Wilander, and Michael

Chang. Offensive players include John McEnroe, Martina Navratilova, Boris Becker, Pete Sampras, and Stefan Edberg.

A defensive strategy can best be described as winning by attrition. The defensive player basically plans to hit one more ball in the court on each point than his opponent. Of course he will knock off an easy winner if the opportunity arises. But most of the time he is as consistent as possible while either waiting for his opponent to miss or while jerking his opponent around the court trying to help him to miss. If his opponent comes to the net, he blunts the attack with lobs or passing shots. His aim is to show his opponent that attacking the net won't work, forcing him back to the baseline for a war of attrition. Bulldog tenacity, conservatism, patience, and concentration are traits associated with the defensive mentality.

In the right hands, a defensive strategy can be diabolical. Imagine, if you will, facing Bjorn Borg in his prime. You would be up against the ultimate in defense. Try to come to the net and you get passed or lobbed. Borg is too fast and accurate to be overpowered by attacking the net. So you stay back and try to rally with him. However, lurking in the back of your mind, as you play point after endless point, is the fact that Borg is in superb physical condition. His heart rate is in the low forties and he is reputed to be tireless. He has been earning a fine living for years by never missing ground strokes, appears unperturbable and infinitely patient. Since Borg won't miss, tire, get bored, or succumb to an attack, you end up simply running out of ideas—checkmate!

Against Borg, most players usually ended up taking wilder and wilder chances, committing more and more errors. To make life even more miserable for his opponents, Borg would continually move them around the court. Since it's obviously more difficult to control the ball when one is scrambling and off balance, Borg forced even more errors from his opponents. He literally wore them down. Physically exhausted, employing a high-risk, low-percentage strategy, his opponents inevitably broke down. And because they believed that Borg did not suffer equally, they were beaten not only physically but mentally.

An offensive strategy, on the other hand, relies on hitting winners or forcing your opponent into a position where he must gamble with a difficult shot to avoid having you put the ball away. In either case the points end rather quickly. Nerve, reflexes, power, speed, and accuracy are key assets for the offensive player.

Most attacking players are net rushers or serve-and-volleyers rather than baseliners. That's because it is clear that good volleyers can consistently hit put-away shots from the net position. It is not clear, at least to me, that many people can consistently put the ball away from the baseline. A very few top male professionals, most notably, Andre Agassi, have been successful going for winners on a regular basis with their ground strokes. And in the women's division, it has been used even more successfully by the likes of Monica Seles, Steffi Graf, and Jennifer Capriati. But in any case it is a very high-risk strategy and I would never even consider it for a player below a national- or world-class tournament standard.

Why is this strategy so difficult? The answer is simple. To put the ball away from the net, you need hit it only twenty to forty feet and it's easy to angle the ball out of the court. You don't need excessive power nor pinpoint accuracy. And because you're closer to your opponent when you hit the ball, you give him less time to react and reach your shot. But from the baseline you have to hit the ball seventy to eighty feet before it gets past your opponent. The angles are also disadvantageous. Therefore, you have to hit the ball extremely hard and close to the lines; otherwise, your opponent has too much time to run the ball down. Only the top tournament players have the tremendous power, control, and nerve to do it with any regularity.

In my mind the jury is still out, even at the highest levels of the game, on whether an attacking player should go for winning ground strokes off of short balls or whether he should use short balls as an avenue to the net and win the point with his volley. At the moment my vote is to attack at the net, although this may change in the future as the top players' ground strokes continue to become more powerful.

Up to now, I have seen a few players consistently end points with ground stroke winners from the baseline, but I have seen a whole lot more do it from the net. At the same time I have seen an awful lot of talented, skillful players try attacking off the ground and go down in flames.

That doesn't necessarily hold true in women's tennis, however. At the tournament level, a baseline attack has certain considerations in its favor. Since women are generally not as quick about the court as men, the aggressive baseliner has certain advantages.

The advantage follows from the general rule that *a successful tennis player must be able to either run or hit*. This means that the slower, less agile player has to hit the ball harder and take more risks than a quicker, more agile player. In this way the slower player can force his opponent to hit his shots off balance and without preparation. And under these circumstances, his opponent will be unable to take advantage of the slower player's lack of mobility.

A quick player, on the other hand, can afford to take less risks because he is able to run down his opponent's shots. However, by the same token, against slower opponents it pays to hit harder and take more risks because you can put them in trouble and hit winners more easily. Though you will make more errors, you will be compensated by hitting more winners. Steffi Graf, Monica Seles, and Jennifer Capriati all win a substantial number of points by hitting ground stroke winners. By contrast, it is more difficult to hit baseline winners in the male professional game because the players can move so quickly.

That's not to say there haven't been many high-ranking male pros who've tried to attack from the baseline. Both Jimmy Arias and Aaron Krickstein had tremendous success at an early age by hitting winners from the backcourt. Both had big forehands and both reached the top ten in the world as teenagers. Arias even won the Italian Championship on slow clay this way. But both subsequently fell in the rankings and languished for years back in the pack. Arias never again reached his former heights. Krickstein, after a long and painful period of adjustment, modified his game under the tutelage of Brian Gottfried and Tim Gullikson.

Though he has made it back into the world's top ten on occasion, he's never really fulfilled his early promise. The question is, why did these young talents, after reaching such heights in tennis at such early ages, falter as they got older rather than continue to develop?

I believe the answer lies in the nature of youth. As teenagers, they had the nerve, fearlessness, and self-confidence to make incredibly difficult shots on a consistent basis. Maybe they just didn't realize how risky it was to whale winners all afternoon from behind the baseline. But it is said of fighter pilots that they are at their best when they are young and full of blind confidence. Age and experience breed conservatism as one learns about all the things that can go wrong.

With the years Krickstein and Arias may simply have lost the reckless abandon required to execute their high-risk strategies successfully. Though both have adjusted their games somewhat and have found a modicum of success, neither has learned to attack at the net. MORAL: If you plan to be an attacking player, work on your volley and overhead. You will need them!

Which strategy is best for you? Start by asking yourself, "Am I able to cover the net and consistently put balls away with volleys and overheads?" If the honest answer is no, you are, like it or not, a defensive player. If you do not play at the highest levels of professional tennis, you should consider winning by attack only if you have a dependable volley and overhead.

In my experience the most common strategic mistake made by recreational players is attempting to be attacking players when they only have the tools to be defensive players. They try to force the play by hitting ground strokes too hard and too close to the lines, so they miss too much. They don't volley well enough to come in and finish points at the net, so they stay back and smack their ground strokes. They hit them so hard they can rarely keep the ball in the court for more than three or four shots a rally. And they never seem to catch on that the percentages are against them. Maybe watching the likes of Andre Agassi and Monica Seles whacking balls on television produces false expectations. The champions have spent a lifetime learning to hit balls near the lines at mach speeds. The normal person is literally playing a different game.

And there is a subtle psychological payoff for adopting the low-percentage strategy of hitting the ball too hard. It lowers your stress during the match and reduces the amount of disagreeable effort you must expend on concentration and willpower. I suspect that we are all aware at some level of consciousness that protracted battles of attrition on the tennis court are tense and unpleasant. Not only are we prone to choke in such situations, but our egos are forced to bear an uncomfortably direct responsibility for any loss. Most people find it more soothing to swat away at the ball and leave their fate in the hands of the gods. Only the winners are determined to control the outcome of the match themselves.

Tennis matches are not won with great shots. They are won with many, many *pretty* good shots. It is like chopping down a tree. You don't do it with one tremendous stroke of the ax. You do it with the accumulated effect of many small strokes. There is no three-point play in tennis, as there is in basketball. You can hit the greatest shot in the world, and you still only get one point for it. And you can nullify this in one second by making an easy error.

In order to win, then, you must have more willpower and concentration than your opponent. This keeps your error rate low. You will ultimately win when your opponent runs out of willpower and his error rate increases. Your main task as a competitor, then, is to maintain your concentration longer than your opponent.

All the great professionals have tremendous willpower and concentration. They can play every point at 100 percent efficiency for four or five hours. This is tremendously difficult. Luckily, you do not have to do this. All you have to do is mentally outlast your opponent, and your opponent is not Jim Courier or Monica Seles. This reminds me of the joke about the two friends who are camping out in the forest. In the middle of the night they are awakened by a huge grizzly bear who is snarling and clawing at the side of their tent, about to break in. In a fright, one says to the other, "We'd better get out of here. Do you think you can outrun the grizzly?" And his friend answers, "I don't have to outrun the grizzly. I just have to outrun you!"

Most players don't realize their strategic shortcomings because most of their opponents make the same mistakes they do. As long as your opponent can't hit the ball in the court more than three or four times per point, it won't be an obvious problem if you can't either. The outcome of such matches is random and usually depends on who happens to hit a few extra balls in on a particular day. (And it makes for good social tennis, since no one can completely dominate.) Only when they play a (dare I say the word?) "dinker" do they have to face the reality of their own ineffectiveness.

The true defensive player (or "dinker," as he is unaffectionately called in recreational circles) is prepared to hit ten, twenty, or more balls in the court per point. It does not take a nuclear physicist to figure out what will happen if a player who misses every third ball meets a player who misses every tenth ball. Unless he can hit a winner on every second ball, the inconsistent player will get slaughtered.

Dinkers are both feared and reviled. Just listen to the common complaints concerning dinkers you're likely to hear at any club:

- Dinkers don't play "right."
- Dinkers will never get any better (while the rest of us, of course, will).
- Losing to a dinker doesn't "count," since he uses an inherently immoral style of play.
- Dinkers are, in fact, cowardly little conservative people—probably accountants or computer programmers.

But dinkers understand the facts of life at the recreational level of tennis. As tennis guru Vic Braden has often pointed out, the defensive player has the advantage at this level of tennis, so it doesn't pay to take a lot of risks. He aptly advises the club player, no matter how much trouble he may be in, to always give his opponent another opportunity to miss. Dinkers frustrate beyond endurance those many players who have not figured this out yet. For every player who thinks he is capable of hitting his shots hard and near the lines, the dinker simply shows him he cannot. Since most players are loath to face this unpleasant reality, they disparage the dinker.

Yet most great champions started out as dinkers when they were young. They wanted to win and immediately understood that winning required consistency. As they grew and their games matured, they began to hit harder and take more risks. Yet because they learned first to be consistent, they were able to develop reliable strokes. It is more effective to learn to hit the ball in the court first and *then* to hit it hard, than to hit it hard and later learn to hit it in. Hitting easy and under control allows you to work out a mechanically sound stroke. Then when you miss you can understand why and make adjustments. But when you slug the ball without proper control, there is a random aspect to your winners and errors. It is very difficult to adjust and correct your strokes because everything happens so quickly. Real understanding of stroke mechanics may never develop.

Learning consistency and control allows you to develop the heart and habits for winning. Jose Higueras, ranked among the top ten players in the world during his illustrious playing career and now coaching champions Michael Chang and Jim Courier, is a stickler for keeping the ball in the court. No matter how much power his players may have or how often they can hit winners, Jose stresses that missing is the cardinal sin. He says that if you miss a lot, you are going to lose no matter how many great shots you make. And Jose hates losing.

As a general rule, you should hit the ball as hard as you can as long as you can keep it in the court all the time. And there is a limit to how hard you can hit before you start to lose control of the ball. All players have only a certain range of comfortable power where they have relatively good control of the ball. Within this range their rate of error will be low. But if they try to play at a power which is above this

THINK TO WIN

range, their rate of error will increase dramatically. Ideally, a player should play most of his shots right at the top of his controllable power range, but never above it. You can certainly work on increasing your power in practice, but in matches you need to do whatever it takes to win. If your control improves enough to allow you to hit harder and still keep the ball in, then by all means do so. Unfortunately, at the lower levels of the game this requires most people to hit the ball much easier than they might like.

This doesn't mean that defensive players should never go for winners. Borg and Evert did so when the opportunity arose. And they certainly jerked their opponents around the court to tire them and help them miss. If the ball is short and high enough, go for the put-away. But the key phrase is *short and high enough.* Like the hungry kid whose eyes are bigger than his stomach, most players overestimate their own abilities in this respect and go for winners too often. They seem oblivious to the fact that when they hit hard and near the lines, their errors generally outnumber their winners. That's why the player who is prepared to hit the ball in the court ten to twenty times per point and makes liberal use of the high lob whenever he gets into trouble is likely to win a lot of matches.

Here's a practical example. Some years ago I injured my right shoulder and had to have an operation. Desperate for exercise while mending, I decided to try playing tennis left-handed. Never having done much with that hand before, I was somewhat uncoordinated and hit the ball very weakly and inaccurately. I found, however, that by hitting the ball fifteen feet over the net and aiming for the middle of the court I would rarely miss.

Yet, to my shock, I was still able to beat all but the very best players at the local tennis club. They hit hard and near the lines. I ran and lobbed. They would miss before I would get tired. Eventually, when they saw they couldn't blow me off the court, we would get into some very long points. Now it became a matter of who was willing to stay out there the longest rather than who could hit the ball the best. In this we were on even terms. They had to be prepared to hit twenty or thirty balls in per point. To do so they couldn't afford to take much risk themselves. Although they could move me a little more than I could move them, it was not enough to make much difference. The issue still would be settled by a battle of wills. And my will was fortified by the fact that I had no alternative. The only type of player who could beat me was one with a good overhead and volley. And those were few at the club level.

That experience taught me much about the mentality of the successful competitor. For the defensive player, especially at the recreational level, it means being willing to stay out there all day until your opponent weakens. It's like winning a water fight in a pool. You splash him, he splashes you. Your eyes begin to hurt, but so do his. Each splash is annoying but not devastating. There is no way for either of you to generate a knockout punch. So you both keep pecking away at each other until one decides the reward is not worth the punishment.

It is only in tournament-level tennis, particularly on fast surfaces, that the advantage actually shifts toward the attacking player. The tournament players are strong, accurate, and fast. They can put the ball away with overheads and volleys. It pays for them to take some risks with their ground strokes, force some short balls, and come in to the net.

The key is whether you have the necessary weapons to attack. At the pro level, offense has the edge in the men's game. In women's tennis, the advantage seems about evenly divided between offense and defense. (Note how evenly Evert and Navratilova were matched in their great rivalry.) In the junior tournaments (under the age of about fourteen or fifteen), the advantage is with defense for either sex.

Successful offense in tennis is similar, in a certain sense, to successful offense in chess. In chess an attack is advisable only if you can marshal enough pieces and power to dominate an area of the board. If you cannot generate enough power to push an attack home completely, it is best not to try it. An attack which falls short merely exposes your pieces, and you ultimately get cut up.

In tennis, offense means attacking at the net with volleys

and overheads. The points will be short and the net player must put the ball away quickly. If he has the tools to do so consistently, offense is a great play. If he doesn't, he exposes himself needlessly to his opponent's passing shots and lobs and ultimately gets beaten.

Offense versus defense. It's one of the great confrontations that makes the game of tennis multidimensional. Now that you understand the way points are won with offense or defense in a match, let's see the specific ways to best implement those two strategies.

BASELINE STRATEGY

3

Okay, you've assessed your strengths and weaknesses. And whether you have concluded that your best overall strategy is offense or defense, you will still spend much of your time on the baseline trading ground strokes with your opponent—waiting for him to either miss or hit a short ball that you can attack. But waiting is not all there is to it. There's a lot you can do to increase your chances of winning the point and your opponent's chances of losing it. Here are the elements that will put the percentages in your favor.

The first basic rule of baseline play is: *The player best able to win crosscourt rallies will probably win the match.* This is because, all else being equal, the safest place to hit ground strokes is crosscourt. Since tennis is a game of errors (that is, the player who makes the most errors usually loses), sophisticated opponents will get into a large number of crosscourt rallies. And if you should turn out to be more consistent at hitting the ball crosscourt than your opponent, you will win most of these rallies. Then what are your opponent's options? He will be forced to try the low-

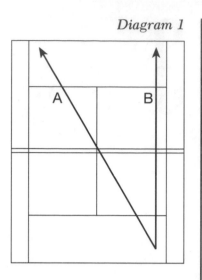

Diagram 1

percentage down-the-line shots too often and ultimately get beaten.

Why is the crosscourt shot safer than down-the-line? There are a number of reasons:

1. The net is lower in the center.
2. The court is longer in the crosscourt direction.
3. You end up in a better geometric position on the court to defend against your opponent's next shot.

Diagram 1 illustrates the first two reasons why you're better off hitting the ball crosscourt. Line A represents a ball hit crosscourt and line B a ball hit down-the-line. Note that A passes over the low part of the net in the middle, while B has to clear the high part at the side. Also note the length of line A is longer than the length of line B, since it is the hypotenuse of a right triangle with line B forming one of the sides. The hypotenuse is always the longest side of a right triangle. This means, of course, you can hit the ball crosscourt farther and still keep it in the court. A crosscourt shot has, therefore, a greater margin for error.

Finally, let's see why hitting crosscourt puts you in a better position to defend against your opponent's next shot. Consider the situation in which your opponent hits a crosscourt forehand that lands deep in your forehand corner, as shown in Diagram 2. What is your highest percentage reply?

Should you hit the ball back crosscourt, right to your opponent, or down-the-line into the open side of the court? (See Diagram 3.)

Diagram 2

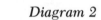

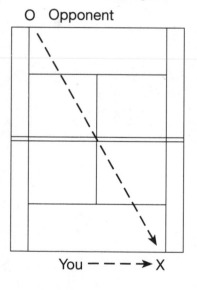

Diagram 3

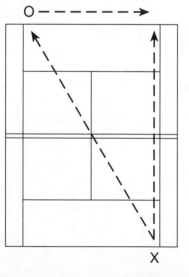

Most players would be tempted to hit into the open court because they would get the immediate gratification of seeing their opponent run across the court for the ball. But this gratification would be short-lived. Unless you hit a winner or near-winner, your opponent now has the advantage of court position. The geometric situation is shown in Diagram 4.

From here your opponent can hit the ball crosscourt and run you out past the sideline. You can only run him a distance C; he can run you a distance D, which is greater. I like his side of the bargain. He runs sooner in the exchange, but you run farther. And if, by the same logic which convinced you to hit down-the-line the first time, you decide to hit down-the-line again, look what happens in Diagram 5.

He runs a distance E to get your shot, and you run a distance F to get his. If you carry this reasoning to its logical conclusion and get into a rally in which he hits every ball crosscourt and you hit every ball down-the-line, the pattern would be as shown in Diagram 6. You would be doing most of the running.

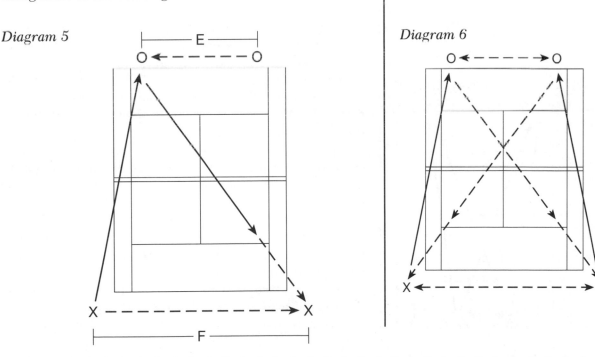

Diagram 4

Diagram 5

Diagram 6

Diagram 7

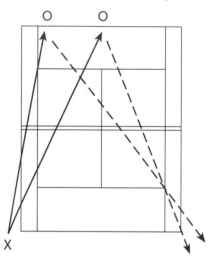

Diagram 8

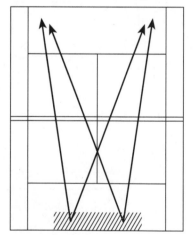

When you are near the sideline and hit the ball down-the-line, you cannot run your opponent any farther than the width of the court. But in hitting crosscourt, he can run you way beyond the sideline. And the closer to the sideline you hit the ball, the wider he can run you. On the other hand, if you hit the ball near the middle of the court, even by hitting the next ball crosscourt he cannot run you very wide at all (see Diagram 7).

Thus, a down-the-line shot hit from near the sideline opens up your court and leaves you exposed. Your opponent can do a number of bad things to you on the next shot. On the other hand, if you are near the center of the court you can hit down-the-line whenever you choose without exposing yourself. A good rule of thumb is to forget about hitting the ball down-the-line whenever your opponent has hit the ball deep and near your sideline. Just go back as deep crosscourt as you can to get yourself out of trouble.

Another general rule for baseline play is that *down-the-line shots should only be used for attack.* Since successful attacking can only be done on a consistent basis off of short balls, hit most deep balls back crosscourt or down the middle.

Balls hit near the center of the court are, in a sense, always being hit crosscourt no matter which sideline they are hit toward. Diagram 8 illustrates this point.

You have a great deal of freedom in choosing where to hit balls which land in the shaded area. No matter which direction you hit, your court is not opened up and the ball travels over the lower part of the net.

If your opponent hits the ball short and sufficiently high, even though it lands near one of your sidelines, you again have great freedom of shot selection. You can attack either down-the-line or crosscourt. But now the down-the-line shot has certain advantages. In this case the fact that you are hitting into the short part of the court actually helps because the distance the ball must travel before getting past your opponent is minimized.

Notice in Diagram 9 the ball is put away once it reaches the shaded area and the shortest distance to the shaded area is along pathway A. For a given velocity of shot your opponent will have the least time to react if it's hit along pathway A.

The basic ground stroke strategy, then, is initially to hit deep or wide crosscourt. If your opponent hits crosscourt and the ball is deep or wide, hit it back crosscourt. If it is short crosscourt you may attack down-the-line or not. If he hits down-the-line, reply with a crosscourt. Basically you should be working deep and crosscourt while waiting for your opponent to expose himself either by hitting short or down-the-line from an improper position. Then you can start to run him. These patterns, of course, are merely general suggestions to increase your percentages. You vary your game around them as the situation dictates.

Whenever your opponent has you in difficulty, send the ball back high and deep. In fact, if you are in enough trouble you can simply lob. This will give you time to recover back to the center of the court and make it difficult for your opponent to hit his next shot hard. Why take chances? Just throw the ball up and start the point over.

If your opponent has hit the ball short and wide, your best reply is as deep as possible crosscourt, even if you have been taken way wide of the court. It may seem as if you will not have enough time to recover, but your opponent's only killing shot would be a half-volley down-the-line, and this is very difficult. He may try it, but the ball will be heading toward the central area of your court rather than beyond your sidelines and you can probably run it down (see Diagram 10).

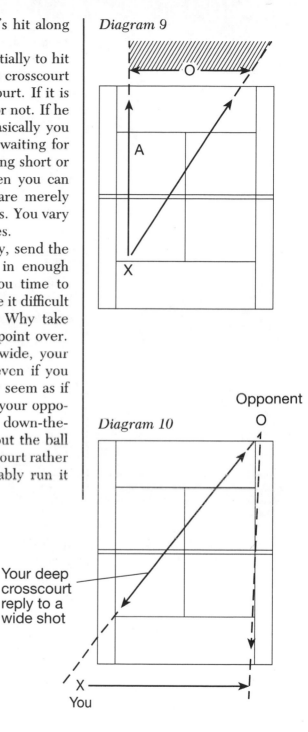

Diagram 9

Diagram 10

Opponent
O

Your deep crosscourt reply to a wide shot

X
You

Don't be tempted to try the down-the-line desperation winner. It's a low-percentage play.

Of course, these basic rules must be modified to keep your opponent guessing and take advantage of opportunities. For example, after you have traded several crosscourts your opponent will start anticipating additional crosscourts and stop moving all the way back to the center. Now a down-the-line can be very damaging. He has been set up and pinned crosscourt. When you finally make your play he will have trouble reaching the ball and be less able to hurt you with a crosscourt reply. Just remember, you can't get hurt hitting an extra ball or two crosscourt, but you can be hurt hitting down-the-line prematurely or off an improper ball.

The foregoing strategies depend on certain underlying assumptions. These are: (1) your opponent's forehand and backhand are about equal; (2) your forehand and backhand are about equal; and (3) you can win the crosscourt rallies. There are some further rules of strategy which, in fact, often supersede the crosscourt strategy, particularly if the assumptions just given do not hold.

1. Use your strengths whenever possible and hide your weaknesses.
2. Avoid your opponent's strengths and exploit his weaknesses.

What do you do, for example, if your opponent has the advantage in the crosscourt rallies on one side? You obviously don't want to get into a lot of exchanges where you are losing most of the points, so as soon as the opportunity arises you must move the ball over to the other wing and get into crosscourt rallies where you have the advantage. But how can you do this without exposing your court?

As soon as your opponent hits a ball anywhere near the middle of the court, hit down-the-line. You may be momentarily exposed to being hurt with a crosscourt reply, but not dangerously so. Because you are near the middle of the court, a few extra steps will move you into position to cover the crosscourt. In essence you trade an extra run for the privilege of exchanging a disadvantageous crosscourt rally for an advantageous one. (And if you are disadvantaged in the crosscourt rallies on both sides, you had better be a very good volleyer.)

When you decide to hit down-the-line to change the crosscourt rally, remember that the closer you are to the sideline, the farther you will have to run to cover your court. This is where being fast on your feet is a tremendous advantage. If you are quick enough, you can afford to hit down-the-line from positions quite far from the center of the court and still scramble back into position.

It is generally easier to cover your court when you hit the forehand down-the-line than when you hit the backhand down-the-line. This is because the footwork involved in hitting the two strokes is different. You should usually hit wide forehands with an open stance. This stance is made with your feet spread parallel to the baseline so that before you begin your backswing you are facing the net. It allows you to immediately push off back to the center of the court with your outside leg.

By contrast, when you hit a backhand, whether you are wide or in the middle of the court, you must use the closed stance. This stance is made with your feet spread perpendicular to the baseline. A line drawn across your toes would point toward the net. It is very awkward to use an open stance when hitting a backhand. You simply cannot bring your shoulders into play properly if you stand facing the net on the backhand.

And this slows your recovery move on the backhand because you must take an extra step in order to bring your legs parallel with the baseline. Only then can you push off with your outside leg and start your move back to the center of the court. This, of course, takes more time.

There are many special situations in which it is advantageous to override the crosscourt strategy. One example is if you just happen to have a darn good down-the-line shot and can hit it hard without missing it too often. Maybe you just happen to be gifted down-the-line. In this case you can simply put your opponent under too much pressure to hurt you. But remember, you are momentarily at a geometric disadvantage in covering your court, so your shot had better be a good one.

Some of the touring professionals can do this and get away with it. In fact, both players are often looking for an opportunity to go on offense and sometimes it is a matter of simply beating the other player to the punch. Although a tough down-the-line shot may be somewhat risky, the pros have found that it is also risky to wait too long and have one's opponent go on offense first. But the average player must be wary of self-delusion. It is certainly satisfying to whack a ball down-the-line and send your opponent scurrying into the corner. But you are playing against the percentages and must be continuously sensitive to balancing errors and ego.

If your opponent is weak on one side, it often pays to open up your court in order to hit into the weak side. He may hit the stroke so badly that he cannot hurt you anyway. And even if he can hurt you a little, you will now be in position to trade crosscourts with his weaker side. The trick, of course, is to get into crosscourt rallies that you can usually win. And if your opponent hits one shot substantially better than the other, only hit into the strong side when he leaves you a lot of room and you can hurt him. Otherwise stick with the weak side.

A common imbalanced case is where a player has a big forehand and weak backhand. If he is smart he will run around his backhand every chance he gets and pound his forehand into your backhand. These rallies progress with him standing in his backhand corner hitting forehands while you try vainly to thread the needle and find his backhand. The usual rally position is shown in Diagram 11.

He hits forehands into your backhand, and you hit backhands into the backhand side of his court. With respect to court position, it is the same as having a backhand-to-backhand crosscourt rally—except he is hitting forehands. Your options are limited. It is very risky to hit your backhand down-the-line into his open court, since it goes right into his big forehand and leaves your court open. At the same time it is hard to hit to his backhand because he has left you so little room. You find yourself vaguely disqui-

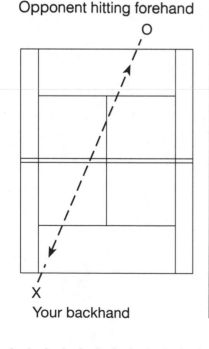

Diagram 11
Opponent hitting forehand

Your backhand

eted, in that he gets to hit the forehand he likes into your backhand all afternoon and there appears to be little you can do about it.

But you can do something. Hit your backhand as deep crosscourt as possible and wait for him to hit short, down the middle or to your forehand. Then try to take him as wide as possible on his forehand side. This exposes his weak backhand. If you can, attack his backhand on the next shot and possibly even come to the net. In fact, he won't like hitting forehands from wide on his forehand side at all. Because most players try to hit to his backhand all the time, he is not used to hitting forehands from this side of the court and will feel uncomfortable. You may even be able to beat him in some forehand crosscourt rallies. But in any case you will disrupt his normal pattern of play. And your brazenness in challenging his powerful forehand may just undermine his confidence.

If your forehand is substantially your stronger side, hit it as often as possible, preferably from your backhand side into your opponent's backhand, so the positions in the scenario I've just described are reversed. If your opponent hits down-the-line into the open court on your forehand side, make an extra effort to hurt him with a deep or sharply angled crosscourt shot. This, hopefully, will scare him away from hitting into your open forehand area and force him to hit into the tiny space available to reach your backhand. Of course, you should work on your backhand in practice, but until it gets more on par with your forehand, hide it in matches and use your forehand.

Finally, keep the ball deep. I cannot emphasize enough the value of depth on your shots! First, if you hit at least halfway between the service line and the baseline, your opponent will have difficulty attacking no matter what advantage he may have in court position. Second, if you hit deep—near the baseline—your opponent will tend to hit short, giving you an opportunity to attack. In fact, depth is an excellent substitute for power. If you had to choose between the two, pick depth every time.

The value of a hard-hit shot is greatly reduced when it lands short. When the ball hits the court, it slows down substantially. Deep balls travel most of their distance through the air at a higher velocity. Once they hit the ground and slow up, they have a relatively short distance to travel before getting past your opponent. Softer, deep balls will often get past an opponent more quickly than hard, short ones because the latter travel too much of their distance after they have bounced and slowed down. Pancho Gonzales was one of the greatest attacking players of all time, yet he rarely hit the ball hard. But he hit it very, very deep. I can still picture Pancho's volley floating deep into the corner as his opponent scurries vainly after it, never quite able to catch up.

In summary, to play the percentages from the baseline, you should:

1. Rally crosscourt
2. Attack down the line
3. Avoid your opponent's strengths and exploit his weaknesses
4. Use your strengths and hide your weaknesses
5. Hit the ball deep

It pays for every player to know how to play percentage tennis from the baseline. Because whether you choose to play offense or defense, the simple fact that you must return serve every other game means that you have to start at least half the points in the match from the baseline. And since effective baseline play depends upon having accurate, powerful, and error-resistant ground strokes, let's take a look at some ground stroke mechanics that will help you develop the strokes you need.

GROUND STROKES | 4

How should you hit your ground strokes? Trying to figure out the best way by watching the top professionals is bewildering because of the tremendous variety of techniques they use. Some hit facing the net, others stand sideways. Some hit with heavy topspin, others hit flat. Some whip the racket around with their arms and wrists, while others use their shoulders and legs. Grips vary all around the racket.

The question is, is proper stroke technique simply a matter of individual preference or are some techniques better for everyone in all cases? I would answer that there are, in fact, easier as well as more difficult ways of hitting the ball. Yet I believe it is always better to perform a physical task in the easiest possible way. The differences in the way professional tennis players hit the ball prove only that great athletes who work hard enough can do things the hard way and still be effective. But even they would have been better off if they had started out doing things the easy way and not wasted their talent and energy making up for inefficient stroke mechanics.

To see what I mean, let's create a simpler game, such as

tossing a tennis ball into the corner wastebasket. Here there are many techniques you could use. You could throw overhand, underhand, sidearm, hook it over your head, behind your back, backhand. It's obvious that throwing overhand is inherently easier than throwing it from behind your back. But if a great athlete practices the behind-the-back shot six hours a day for ten years, he is likely to be better at throwing it that way than you are throwing over-hand. That doesn't mean that you should throw it behind your back too. As great as the pro may be, he would have been even better if he had learned to throw overhand in the first place.

Proper stroking technique can be determined by analyz-ing exactly what one is attempting to accomplish with a particular stroke. Anything you do on the court must have some logical function and help you in some way. With ground strokes, you ideally wish to generate maximum power *and* control the angle of the racket face as well as the racket's path of motion. The problem is that these are in-herently antagonistic goals. The more power one produces, the less control one has.

Let's explore why. Power can be directly related, in a simple sense, to the velocity of the racket in the direction of the shot at the moment of impact. All else being equal, the faster your racket is moving, the harder you will hit the ball. Since the ball must be hit a long distance (often in excess of seventy feet) and has already bounced (thereby slowing down and losing energy), a great deal of energy must be transferred to the ball by the racket.

However, you have maximum control of the racket when it is still. If you just held it out to your side and didn't move it, the racket face would remain in whatever position you put it and its path of motion would obviously be stable since it isn't moving. Whether it is set slightly open (racket face tilted upward), slightly closed (racket face tilted down-ward), or flat (racket face perpendicular to the ground), it will remain that way. A ball that strikes it in the center will always bounce off it in a predictable way. When you don't move the racket, you have total control (since the racket remains in the position you originally set), but you impart zero energy to the ball. Once you move the racket, it starts to wiggle around and the exact angle of the racket face can change slightly from what you originally set. That's the same thing as saying you lose some control.

The ball, by the way, is interested only in how fast the racket is moving, not *how* it is moved. For example, if you stuck your racket out the window of a train moving sixty miles an hour and it struck the ball, the ball would find that indistinguishable from a normal ground stroke where you swung the racket sixty miles an hour. Sixty miles an hour is sixty miles an hour, no matter how you get it. (It may, however, be somewhat impractical to drive a train around the tennis court.) Since one strives to get maximum racket velocity with a minimum of instability, how that velocity is achieved makes a great deal of difference to the player.

There are four basic sources of power—four ways to move the racket in the direction of the hit. Each is a trade-off between power and control. But by combining elements of each technique into your ground strokes, you can tailor your shots to balance power and control to meet the needs of the situation on court.

The first source of power is to move the racket with the legs. Hold the racket out to your side, set the angle to the racket face, and simply step in the direction you wish the ball to go. The racket, obviously, moves forward with you. It doesn't move very fast, but nonetheless it moves and thereby gives you power. At the same time you will lose virtually no control, since, relative to you, the racket is really being held stationary. The angle of the racket face remains at whatever angle you originally set it.

You may be able to move the racket five to six miles per hour just by using your legs. Since a tournament player ultimately achieves racket velocities in the range of fifty to a hundred miles per hour on ground strokes, he can add about 5 percent to the power of his shots just by stepping forward as he hits. You can certainly do without it, but since it comes at virtually no cost in terms of control loss, it always pays to step into the ball as you hit.

The second source of power—and second best in terms of racket head control—comes from rotating the shoulders and upper body. To demonstrate this, simply hold the racket out to your side with your elbow tight against your body. Now lock your arm in place at the shoulder and rotate your upper body from the waist. The racket moves, giving you power. The racket face also tends to remain very stable during the movement. Whatever angle you initially set the racket face at remains fixed as you move your racket by shoulder rotation.

The third source of power comes from moving the arm relative to the shoulder. To demonstrate this, hold the racket out to your side and swing your arm back and forth while holding the rest of your body immobile. Again the racket moves, giving you power, but this time the source of power is more unstable. Notice how the racket face wiggles around as you swing your arm. If you were initially to set the racket face at a forty-five-degree angle, it would be difficult to keep it precisely that way throughout the movement.

The fourth and final source of power is to move the racket with the wrist. Demonstrate this principle by holding the racket out to your side, locking your elbow against your body and waving the racket back and forth using only your wrist. Keep your arms, legs, and torso stationary. Notice again the instability in the angle of the racket face during the racket's motion. As it does when swinging with the arm, the racket wiggles around, making precise control difficult.

It may seem picayune, but even small variations in the angle or tilt of the racket face make a great deal of difference as to where the ball will land. Tennis is the most difficult racket sport because of the leverage in the game. By this I mean that the racket is large and the distance the ball travels is relatively long. A variation of only one-eighth of an inch in the angle of the racket face will be magnified by projecting this angular error over the long distance the ball must travel and change where the ball lands by many feet. (By contrast, in racquetball the paddle is shorter and the distances are less, so the angle of the paddle is less critical. This makes it an easier game.) In tennis, fortunately or unfortunately, the angle of the racket face must be controlled with great precision. And this makes tennis a very difficult game to learn.

When you actually hit a ground stroke, you use all four sources of power simultaneously. The ultimate velocity of the racket is the sum of the individual components of velocity contributed by the four sources of power. For example, if you wanted to hit the ball as far as possible, you would use each source to its maximum. You would run as fast as possible in the direction of the ball, rotate your shoulders around like a javelin thrower, pivot, fling your arm forward, and snap your wrist as you hit the ball. You certainly would give the ball a good whack, but I wouldn't bet on hitting anything smaller than the side of a house.

On every shot, you will vary the amount of power you get from the four sources. If you want to maximize control, use your legs and shoulder rotation as much as possible and your arm and wrist as little as possible. If you need to hit the ball harder, use a little more arm or wrist, but be aware that you lose some control of your shot in doing so. Remember too that the power which does not come from one of the sources must come from the other three. You could therefore hit the ball while stepping backward but make up for it by using your arm, shoulder rotation, and wrist more. (For you physicists, in this case, Velocity [racket] − Velocity [pivot] + Velocity [arm] + Velocity [wrist] − Velocity [legs].) Again, the ball does not know what makes the racket move. It knows only velocity, racket angle, and trajectory.

Since your basic objective on ground strokes is to get maximum power *and* maximum control, the ideal stroke should obtain as much power as possible from the legs and shoulder rotation, and as little as practical from the arm and wrist. Jimmy Connors does that about as well as anybody. He simply approaches the ball with his back turned slightly toward the net. Then he throws his weight forward and pivots, with his arms somewhat immobilized at the shoulder. The stroke resembles one of those mechanical hockey games where a metal ball is hit by a rotating hockey stick

FIGURE 1.
Forehand ground stroke.

1   2

activated by a button. If the button is hit at the right time, the ball always goes in the right direction, because no other parts move.

To hit a mechanically sound ground stroke, approach the ball as Connors does, with your shoulders rotated away from the net such that your opponent can see a partial view of your back. In order to look at the ball in this position, you must turn your head so your chin is close to or touching your shoulder. You should resemble a coiled spring (see Figure 1).

Now initiate the stroke by throwing your weight forward into the ball and uncoiling your upper body. The arm and wrist follow in sequence as needed, ideally as little as possible. If the arm is kept relaxed and passive, it will be flung forward with sufficient velocity by the legs and shoulder pivot.

At the higher levels of the game the wrist tends to be used more than would seem warranted, given the loss of control involved. Using the wrist does, however, have certain advantages. It allows great flexibility and deception and can generate power from awkward, off-balance posi-

4

tions. The pros have very strong wrists and are willing to trade some control for these benefits. The use of the arm, on the other hand, can be almost completely replaced by the use of the legs and shoulder rotation. Other than providing maximum power, it has few redeeming virtues and should be reduced as much as possible.

A stroke that gets a large percentage of its power from the legs and shoulders will be compact. The backswing will be short and will be accomplished more by turning the shoulders than by taking the arm back. The ball will be hit harder than is apparent to your opponent because he sees only the short backswing and does not notice that the stroke is being hit from a moving platform. He is surprised by the "heaviness" of the ball because it arrives faster than expected and rushes him. (Actually, folk wisdom says that getting your "weight" into your shot gives you a "heavier" ball, and there is the inference that a 300-pound man stepping into his shot gets more additional power than a 150-pound man. But that is meaningless. There is no such thing as "heaviness" in the ball, there is only velocity and spin, and the benefit of stepping into the shot comes only from

1   2   3   4

FIGURE 2.
Ground stroke off a deep ball.

the velocity of the step, not the weight of the person stepping.) Again, stepping into the ball provides a small but measurable component of racket velocity which is virtually free in terms of loss of racket head control.

This type of stroke works only if you have the proper preparation and position. The ball should be hit relatively close to your body. If the ball is struck too far away, you will have to use too much arm and wrist, and the stroke will become unstable. Incidentally, that is one good reason for running your opponent around. If he can't get to the ball and set up properly, he will be forced to reach and slap at it with his arm and wrist. And that will increase his errors.

Proper preparation means taking the racket back and turning the shoulders early. The backswing should be completed *before the ball bounces on your side of the court!* I cannot stress this strongly enough. Many players wait until the ball bounces before starting their backswing. This is not a problem if the ball is short and slow. But it leads to big trouble on hard, deep shots. The player is forced to step backward and swipe at the ball with his arm and wrist. The proper way to handle deep balls is to take a short, early backswing and step forward into the ball, as in Figure 2.

As a general rule, the deeper or harder your opponent hits the ball, the shorter your backswing should be. This is

THINK TO WIN

because the shorter backswing increases your control, although it costs you some power. When you are facing deep or hard shots, trading some power for more control is a good bargain.

When you are on the run, make sure your backswing is complete before the last step or two. Take long strides to reach the ball; then, with your shoulders already turned, shorten your last few steps as you near the ball (see Figure 3).

FIGURE 3.
Running ground stroke.

1

2

3

4

5

6

FIGURE 4.
(1) Open stance.

1

(2) Closed stance.

2

The question often arises as to whether it is better to hit forehands with an open or closed stance. A player who hits with an open stance has his legs parallel to the net and begins his preparation facing the net. A player who hits with a closed stance stands with his legs perpendicular to the net and begins his preparation sideways to the net. The two stances are shown in Figure 4.

The trouble with the open stance is that you cannot throw your weight forward in the direction of the hit. If you try, you would simply fall on your face, since you have no leg to land on. Since you cannot use your legs for power in an open stance, you must use your arm or wrist more, hence slightly reducing your control.

I recommend using the open stance on forehands only when you are pulled out wide, near or past the sideline. An open stance allows you to save a step and get back to the center of the court more quickly. The trade-off of control for mobility is, in this instance, a good one. But around the center of the court there is no need to make this trade. Even on wide balls, if I were going for a single-shot winner and didn't need to recover, I would try to throw my weight into the court with a closed stance.

The forward movement of the racket on ground strokes should be from low to high. High or circular backswings on the forehand are the norm and fine as long as the racket head drops down below the level of the ball before starting its forward motion. If you take this kind of backswing, there is a trick to ensure that you get your shoulders turned properly. Keep your free hand on the throat of the racket as you take it back, and it will pull your shoulders around during the backswing. (Ilie Nastase, among others, did this effectively.) Once the shoulders are turned, you can release the racket with your free hand and initiate the stroke.

What grip should you use? The pros use every kind of grip, from the most common to the most extreme. I recommend that you use a grip that basically aligns the racket face parallel to the palm of your hand at contact in such a way that both are perpendicular to the ground. On the forehand this is consistent with an Eastern or semi-Western grip.

THINK TO WIN

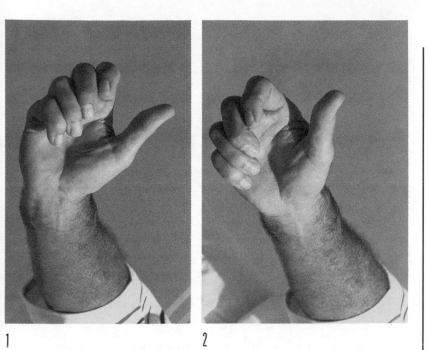

1   2

FIGURE 5.
(1, 2) Wrist movement
with Western grip.

One forehand grip that I feel you should avoid is a Continental grip. Your hand is on top rather than behind the racket and the grip lacks stability. Strokes made with this grip tend to be wristy and, worse still, the particular wrist movement is biomechanically weak as compared to a similar movement made with a semi-Western grip. You simply have more physical strength to move your wrist forward with a semi-Western grip than you do with a Continental grip. In Figure 5 you can see the difference in these two wrist movements.

(3, 4) Wrist movement
with Continental grip.

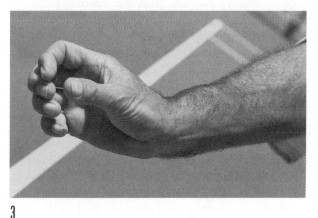

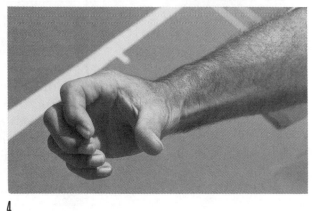

3   4

1 2 3 4

FIGURE 6.
Backhand ground stroke.

For a flat or topspin backhand, you need to use a different grip because the contact point with the ball is different from the forehand. If you use an Eastern forehand grip, you need to rotate the racket handle clockwise between one-half and three-quarters of an inch to obtain the proper backhand grip. This change is necessary so that the palm will again become flat when the racket face is flat.

My experience with the one-handed backhand has been that there is less leeway with the grip than there is with the forehand, and the grip should be pretty close to that just described. A slice backhand can be hit most effectively with a Continental grip, which is about halfway between the backhand and Eastern forehand grips.

Both backhand and forehand ground strokes should be hit in the same basic manner, with maximal use of the legs and shoulder rotation and minimal use of arm and wrist. Figure 6 shows the proper backhand stroke.

There are, however, certain basic physical differences between the two strokes which must be noted to fully understand them. The anatomy of our arm makes us far stronger on the forehand side than on the backhand. To illustrate this, move your wrist forward as you would when hitting a forehand (see Figure 7).

THINK TO WIN

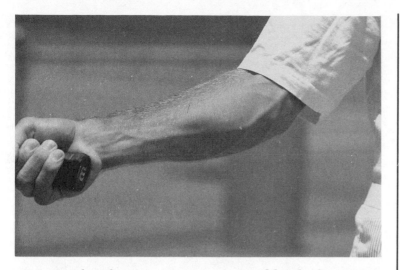

FIGURE 7.
Muscle used with forehand.

Notice that the movement is powered by the large muscle on the inside of the forearm. Now move your wrist backward as you would when hitting a backhand (see Figure 8).

Notice how the wrist is moved on the backhand by the small muscle on the top of the forearm near the elbow. This muscle is many times smaller (hence many times less powerful) than the muscle used on the forehand. We are therefore much stronger physically on our forehands than our backhands.

FIGURE 8.
Muscle used with backhand.

FIGURE 9.
Poked backhand.

1   2

When a person who has never played tennis before first picks up a racket, he has a natural tendency to generate power by just using his arm muscles. The good athlete who wants to have some control right away generally dispenses with the shoulder turn on the forehand and just pokes at the backhand, sticking his elbow out and using his triceps muscle (see Figure 9).

Initially, hitting the ball with his arm gives the beginner maximal control over his strokes because our muscles contain receptive nerves called proprioceptors which notify our brains of the exact position of a limb when we move it. The beginner knows immediately where the racket is at all times during the stroke when he muscles it around. Unfortunately, this doesn't work well in the long run. In particular, the muscles used on the backhand side are too weak to ever generate enough power for a strong stroke. A good backhand requires that you use shoulder rotation and develop some degree of proper stroke mechanics on this side.

Yet at first it feels very insecure to relax your arm and power your backhand by flinging your limp arm forward with your legs and shoulder rotation. A loose arm does not, initially, give one that comforting sense of knowing exactly where one's arm is as it moves. In fact, if a beginner tries to hit his backhands hard this way, he won't know if the ball is going in the court, into the net, or over the fence. Initially you have to hit the ball very easy and very far away from the lines and net because your control is so limited. Practice will eventually give you both power and control because you will learn to power the backhand with the proper sources—*not* the arm. For this reason the backhand often becomes a particularly consistent stroke.

The forehand, by contrast, can be hit quite hard using the arm muscles alone. You do not absolutely *have* to use your legs and shoulders for power. Too often an excessive component of arm power remains in the developed stroke, leading to an unstable stroke. The forehand is a more flexible stroke than the backhand and, with a strong wrist and arm, can be hit powerfully and deceptively even from awkward positions. But because they often rely too much on their arm to power the shot, top players tend to make more errors off this side as well. In my experience with top college players, the forehand will be the more unstable side about 75 percent of the time.

At the higher levels of the game, the forehand is often called a "confidence" shot. This means that players can do a lot of damage with their forehands when they feel confident, but that their forehands can totally break down if they become fearful. Their backhands, on the other hand, tend to be more technically sound and fall apart less frequently.

The normal physiological weakness on the backhand side can be counteracted by hitting with two hands. Not only does this increase a player's strength, but it also guarantees he will rotate his upper body for power, since his shoulders are pulled around when the racket is taken back with both hands on it. This type of backhand tends to be stable and powerful. Unfortunately, once again there is no free lunch. You sacrifice almost a foot of reach in using the extra hand, so a two-fisted player must run farther and work harder to cover the court.

The two-handed backhand is also a somewhat inflexible

stroke. Balls hit directly at the body, extremely low, or extremely high are difficult to handle. It is also hard to hit slice or approach with two hands. Finally, it is difficult to be an effective volleyer with two hands. And using the extra hand on ground strokes retards strength development in the dominant hand. If the player tries to learn a one-handed backhand volley (as he should if he plans to cover the net well), a weak wrist can cause substantial problems unless it is strengthened with extra work.

However, I am not inclined to make a strong case for choosing one of these backhands over the other. Great players have used them both with equal effectiveness. I would, however, highly recommend that if a player chooses a two-handed stroke, he learn to hit wide balls with one hand if the occasion demands. Pancho Segura, the great champion from Ecuador during the 1950s and 1960s, played with two hands on both the forehand and backhand sides, but he volleyed and played wide balls comfortably with one hand. Maybe that is the best of all worlds.

MAKING THE BEST USE OF SPIN

5

Ground strokes can be hit basically three ways: flat (with no spin), with topspin, or with backspin (commonly called slice). Each offers its own unique set of advantages and disadvantages. Though no one shot is ideal to use in all situations, the complete player can benefit by becoming adept at executing all three.

In the 1970s a number of champions began to use heavy topspin on their ground strokes and completely dominated the game. People began to think that using topspin was the best thing to happen to the world since the discovery of fire. More sober analysis has shown it to be useful, but not quite *that* useful. Topspin imparts negative lift to the ball—in other words, it makes the ball drop faster than it would if it were just under the influence of gravity. This provides an extra margin of safety when exchanging ground strokes because the ball can be hit hard, high over the net, and still drop down into the court. In addition, when the ball strikes the court, it bounces higher than normal, often at or above shoulder height, and makes it difficult for your opponent to attack you.

47

FIGURE 10.
Topspin forehand.

1   2

Topspin's greatest value, however, is probably for passing shots. The ball's spin allows it to be hit hard yet still drop down into the court. That's ideal to get the ball past a player at the net, particularly on sharply angled passing shots. Without topspin there is no other way to attain high velocity, clear the net, and put the ball into the short areas of the court. In addition, a ball hit with topspin is difficult to volley because it drops quickly below the level of the net.

The proper technique for hitting a topspin ground stroke is shown in Figure 10.

As you can see, there are some key factors to the mechanics of hitting topspin:

1. The knees are bent initially but straighten out during the course of the stroke. This causes the racket head to rise as it moves forward, and that imparts topspin to the ball.

2. The swing is somewhat longer and more arm and

3   4   5

wrist are used than with a flat stroke. This is necessary because you generally must generate more racket head speed to hit topspin.

3. The ball must be contacted farther in front of your body than with sliced or flat strokes. It is very difficult to put topspin on balls that are struck late.

But for all its advantages, topspin has disadvantages as well. It is an inefficient way to give the ball velocity. Hitting with heavy topspin demands a great deal of effort to move the ball through the air with adequate speed. In simplistic terms, think of the energy being transferred to the ball as being divided into two components: (1) the kinetic energy of the moving ball (velocity), and (2) the rotational energy of the spinning ball (spin). With a flat stroke, all the energy of the swing is transferred into kinetic energy (velocity), and none is siphoned off into spin. That means that you don't have to swing as violently with a flat stroke to hit a hard shot. But because so much energy goes into imparting spin on a topspin stroke, you have to swing very hard to put adequate speed on the ball. And this takes a great deal of strength.

A second difficulty with topspin strokes is that they are easier to mishit than flat strokes. On flat strokes, the racket moves straight through the ball, so the ball "sees" the full face of the racket throughout the swing. It's not difficult to make proper contact in this case. On topspin strokes, on the other hand, the racket moves sharply from low to high, and the ball "sees" only the top edge and partial face of the racket throughout the swing. This sliver of the racket face is essentially a smaller target, so proper contact becomes more tenuous.

A third disadvantage of heavy topspin is that the depth of the shot is more difficult to control. With a flat stroke, depth basically is determined by only two variables: the velocity and trajectory of the racket at impact. (This simplistically ignores such factors as wind resistance, ball weight, and string tension, which we assume to be constant no matter what type of stroke you hit.) This is like an artillery shell for which range is determined by the muzzle velocity of the shell and the elevation angle of the barrel. But with topspin a third variable enters the equation. This is the proportion of energy that goes into velocity versus the proportion that goes into spin. If you come up the back of the ball too sharply, your shot will have more spin and less velocity than intended and fall short. If you strike the ball too flush, it will have more velocity and less spin and carry too deep. Because with topspin you are dealing with three variables instead of two, you must leave more margin for error and keep the ball farther away from the baseline.

When he was reigning world champion, Jimmy Connors, one of the greatest flat ground strokers of all time, used to say that he enjoyed playing Bjorn Borg because Borg hit the ball so short. He said he loved pounding the steady diet of short, high balls that Borg provided. (He didn't enjoy it so much a few years later, when he was a step slower and Borg, in the process of winning Wimbledon five times in a row, was running all his shots down.)

Connors did, in fact, have a wonderful style for playing

Borg, Guillermo Vilas, and other topspin artists because his ground strokes were so deep and efficient. He used to run these opponents around the court until their tongues hung out and eventually finish them off with his volleys. Connors was not as good an athlete as Borg, nor did he put in as many hours on the practice courts, but he was able to beat Borg for many years because his technique gave him a substantial advantage. The power and depth of Connors's ground strokes allowed him to dominate play from the base-line as no one else had done since the days of Don Budge.

I generally advise players to use the flat ground stroke in baseline exchanges because, as mentioned earlier, it can be hit consistently deep, is less subject to mishits, and re-quires a minimum of effort to generate adequate velocity. I am, by the way, using the term *flat* ground stroke to in-clude ground strokes which have a small amount of topspin on them. Thus, I would characterize players like Andre Agassi, Ivan Lendl, and Monica Seles as flat ground strok-ers even though they generally apply some light topspin to the ball. This type of stroke allows its practitioners a better opportunity of gaining control of a point than does heavy topspin, which is most often associated with defensive play-ers.

On the other hand, there will always be particular days or situations when one is short of confidence or control of one's flat strokes. At these times you can add extra topspin and net clearance to all your shots for safety. Though you will have to play a more defensive game and probably will have to do more running, it certainly beats missing.

Backspin or slice is another valuable addition to your shot repertoire. Backspin produces lift, increasing the ball's tendency to remain in the air. Its action counteracts gravity and makes the ball tend to float or sail. (When slice is applied vigorously enough it can even make the ball rise.) One of the best uses of backspin is to get you out of trouble. It can be hit in an emergency with a minimum of prepara-tion and effort. This makes it ideal for those situations in which you are scrambling off balance or in an awkward position and you're not able to set up and hit an ordinary ground stroke. A flick of the wrist can sail the ball back

FIGURE 11.
Backhand slice.

1   2

deep into your opponent's court and give you time to recover.

Slice is especially useful when you have been run out to the end of your reach, particularly on your backhand side. From that position there is often nothing else you can do. A flat or topspin drive might allow you to take the offense and be a better shot if you were able to hit it, but sometimes this is just not possible or has too great a risk of error. Be aware, however, that a defensive slice will generally grab and sit up when it hits the court, giving your opponent the opportunity to hit a strong drive and remain on the offensive. That's why you must hit this slice deep crosscourt if you hope to escape from trouble.

But slice can also be used to create difficulties for your opponent if you can make it skid when it hits the court rather than bounce up. This type of shot will not slow up when it lands. Instead it will stay low and move quickly. This is because the coefficient of sliding friction is much lower than the coefficient of rolling friction. In essence, the skidding ball acts as if the court had suddenly become very slippery and fast.

Any ball can be made to skid on any surface if its trajectory is rather flat and enough backspin is applied. Backspin increases the velocity of the ball's surface relative to the court, and the ball skids when its surface velocity relative to the court is sufficiently high. It is like applying the brakes

3   4

in a car. If the car is moving slowly, the tires will grab and
it will stop immediately. But if it gets moving fast enough
it will skid. And this happens regardless of how good the
tires are or how rough the tarmac may be. Conditions of
good traction merely mean that the car has to be moving
faster before it will skid. The same principles apply on the
tennis court. If the surface is rough, the court will play slow
because it will be difficult to make the ball skid. The ball
will tend to grab and slow down unless it is hit sharply, with
a very flat trajectory and a great deal of backspin.

Slice is often useful when executing backhand approach
shots. (Slice can be used on forehand approach shots as
well, but, as will be described in a later chapter, a short,
flat stroke is usually the shot of choice.) Approach shots are
often hit on the move off low, awkward balls, and a slice
provides the flexibility required in these situations. Here it
is particularly helpful if you can make the ball skid. This
forces your opponent to hit the passing shot off of a low,
fast-moving ball rather than one that is sitting up.

The technique for hitting an effective slice backhand is
shown in Figure 11.

Notice several crucial factors:

1. The knees are bent at the outset and stay bent
throughout the stroke.

2. The racket starts only slightly above the contact

point and basically is swung level through the shot, rather than on a severe high-to-low path.

3. Body weight is thrown forward as the ball is hit.

4. The wrist is cocked in preparation for the stroke and snapped to the straight position at contact with the ball.

Using the wrist is necessary in executing an effective slice approach shot because without it, insufficient backspin will be applied and the ball cannot be made to skid. Sliced backhands hit with a locked wrist tend to sit up and make an easy target for your opponent's passing shot.

Once you master the technique, sliced backhands are easy and fun to hit. You may be tempted to hit them often in backhand exchanges on the baseline even when it would have been perfectly comfortable to hit flat or topspin backhands. That is a mistake, in my opinion. Slice strokes cannot be hit as hard as flat or topspin strokes. If you use them too often you allow your opponent too many opportunities to take control of the point and put you in awkward positions. You will end up on the defense too often. Your basic ground stroke of choice should be a flat or light topspin shot, with the slice being used for an occasional change of pace, to extricate yourself from trouble or to approach on a short ball.

VOLLEY

Few players are *both* great volleyers and great ground strokers. Even world champions have tended to specialize in one to the detriment of the other. To the good fortune of spectators, this has led to some classic rivalries between players of opposing styles, such as Chris Evert–Martina Navratilova and Bjorn Borg–John McEnroe. But did you ever ask yourself why great athletes like Borg and Evert did not simply practice their volleys more and develop great net games to go with their great ground strokes? Or why McEnroe and Navratilova never managed to improve their ground strokes to the level of their volleys?

It was not for lack of trying or willingness to work. The fact is that these players knew the value of improving a deficiency and undoubtedly spent plenty of time trying. But the fundamental concepts of the volley and ground strokes are, in many ways, antagonistic. The strokes are designed to accomplish totally different goals. The rules of one are often exactly reversed for the other.

For example, the ground stroker must generate a great deal of racket-head speed for power, yet control the angle

Diagram 12

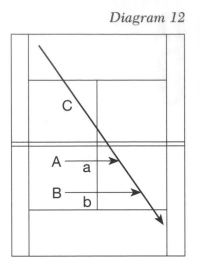

of the racket face and resulting trajectory of the ball with great precision. This requires him to arrive in position to hit the ball early, stop, step up a stationary base, and rotate forward into the ball. The ground stroker is like a battleship firing a salvo—he wants *stability and power*.

The volleyer's task is quite different. Power is not a major issue. The ball has not yet bounced and slowed down, so it still retains most of its original energy. Not much need be added by the volleyer to give the ball adequate velocity. Also, the distance a volley needs to travel is short relative to a ground stroke. A volley can be hit for a winner in twenty or thirty feet, while a ground stroke usually has to travel in excess of seventy feet. The volleyer, therefore, does not have to worry about getting his racket moving at high speed before impact. His main problem is *position on the court*.

If a volleyer could stand within inches of the net, any volley would be easy to knock off. From the service line, however, any volley is difficult, no matter how high or slow the ball is. Close in, the volleyer can hit down on most balls. Once a ball drops below the level of the net, the volley must be hit up to clear the net and relatively softly to stay in the court, and a put-away becomes very difficult. In addition, from near the net the volleyer has a wider selection of angles to hit a winning shot, and it's easier to reach passing shots and cover the net (see Diagram 12).

Note that for a passing shot traveling on path C, a volleyer standing farther from the net at position B must move a distance *b* to intercept it, whereas a volleyer standing at position A need move only a shorter distance *a* to reach the ball.

So why not just stand right next to the net all the time? Because your opponent obviously will lob over your head. The threat of the lob forces the volleyer to wait at a safer position (see Diagram 13) until his opponent has committed to hitting a passing shot rather than a lob.

Once the volleyer sees his opponent committed to hitting a passing shot, he must move forward as fast and far as possible in order to intercept the ball closer to the net. If a very slow ground stroke is hit, the volleyer may be able to

Diagram 13

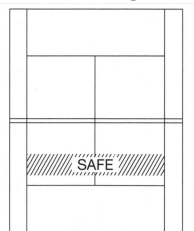

SAFE

sprint all the way up to the net. In this case he will get a relatively high, easy volley from close in and will be moving at high speed when he hits it. This is called "running through the volley"—no effort is made to slow down before contact, and the shot is hit on the run. Running through the volley does not make executing the shot easier—in fact it makes it substantially more difficult. But I advise running through the volley in this situation because it is the only way that you can get as close to the net as possible prior to contact. If you stop before you hit the volley, you will lose several feet of closing distance.

If the passing shot is hit hard and low, the volleyer should move slowly at contact. He won't have time to accelerate and close in very far anyway because the ball will be upon him so quickly. And the difficulty of the shot makes it needlessly risky to execute the volley while running at high speed. However, the volleyer should not stand completely still at contact. Instead, he should *move* into the volley as opposed to running through it. Generally, a volleyer should not try to put this volley away. In compensation, the volleyer will not have moved dangerously close to the net and should be able to retreat comfortably if the next shot is a lob.

On the other hand, a volleyer should do his utmost to put away any slow, hanging passing shot. In this case, he will have charged far past the point of recovery and will be extremely vulnerable to the lob if his opponent reaches his volley. Yet it is the correct gamble. It is too late to become conservative. Once the volleyer ventures forward to the net, he has committed to end the point in a shot or two. The volleyer must seize this golden opportunity by dashing forward in an all-out effort for the kill. Sluggish movement and a cautious volley here will present another opportunity for his opponent to hit a passing shot and is a losing percentage play.

In any case, the net player must develop the mind-set of contacting the volley as close to the net as possible once he knows his opponent has chosen to pass rather than lob. Each additional foot he can close opens up more opportunities for a winning volley. It is not a question of simply

. . . .

closing all the way to the net or not. It is a question of the volleyer instinctively moving forward and picking up every inch of closing distance he can on each volley. A yard is better than a foot, a foot is better than an inch, and an inch is better than nothing.

Movement, then, is an intrinsic part of the volley stroke. (In fact, one way to teach beginners to volley is to have them hold the racket out in front of them and simply run into the ball.) Here is where the volley lies in diametric opposition to the ground stroke. On a volley, you generally hit from a moving platform. On a ground stroke, you stop, set up, and hit from a stationary platform. The volley requires flexibility and quick reactions. The ground stroke demands preparation and stability.

One problem ground strokers have at the net is that they often try to stop and set up a stable base the way they do on the baseline. This limits their flexibility and prevents them from closing to the net. On the other hand, the volleyers often have the opposite problem on the baseline in that they often fail to set up a stationary base for their ground strokes. The volleyer subconsciously learns to incorporate leg movement into his strokes (or at least does not concern himself with getting rid of it), while the ground stroker subconsciously learns to remove leg movement from his strokes. Hence Chris Evert looked awkward and stiff at the net (despite, I am sure, countless hours of practicing the volley), while Navratilova, who is smooth and flexible, never looked as mechanically sound on ground strokes as her great rival.

The volley stroke itself is hit from high to low with a short, jabbing action. The power comes from the wrist, arm, legs, and a small shoulder turn. There is very little if any backswing, with the racket traveling mostly forward and only slightly down. Since the volleyer will be moving forward at a relatively high velocity when he hits the ball and, with a volley, the total velocity of the racket at impact will generally be rather low, the volleyer's legs will contribute a large percentage of the total power needed for the stroke. A long swing, then, becomes superfluous. (With a volley, for example, the racket may be moving somewhere

1

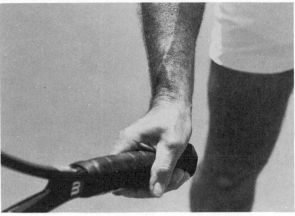

2

between ten and twenty-five miles per hour at contact. Since the volleyer can move forward at speeds approaching ten miles per hour, you can see that in some instances he hardly needs to swing at all.)

High volleys should be hit flat and with a *slightly* longer swing to help put them away. Volleys at net level should be hit with some backspin, and the lower the ball drops, the more backspin you should apply to the ball to help it clear the net. (Like the chip shot in golf, you make the ball go up, paradoxically, by swinging down.)

At more advanced levels, the use of the wrist and arm become more important in hitting the volley. The wrist initially is laid back slightly (see Figure 12) and snapped forward at impact.

FIGURE 12.
(1, 2) Forehand volley wrist movement.

(3, 4) Backhand volley wrist movement.

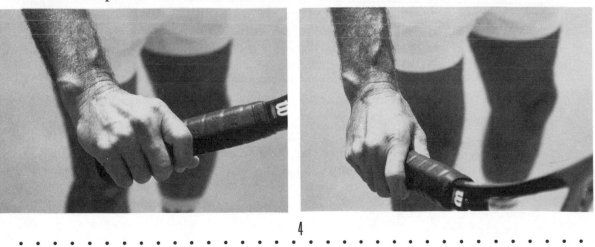

3

4

Wrist and arm action becomes necessary at the higher levels of the game because many volleys are hit lunging at the end of one's reach or from other awkward positions. Although these are difficult sources of power to control, when leaping toward the sideline after a passing shot you simply cannot bring shoulder rotation or leg drive into play. Your wrist and arm are all you have left.

In addition, because the action at the net is so fast and there is usually no time to set up, flexibility becomes a crucial factor. And the wrist is a very flexible source of power. The great volleyers all had great wrists. Billie Jean King, Rod Laver, Pancho Gonzales, John McEnroe, and Martina Navratilova could snap volleys with their wrists from any position on the court to any other spot. McEnroe has been said to have wonderful "hands," which is really tennis talk for wrists. McEnroe's wrists give him incredible flexibility, control, and deception on the volley.

On high volleys, the wrist is snapped sharply for power. On low volleys, you generally should use a "softer" or more supple wrist. Because on low balls you must lift the volley over the net and still bring the ball down into the court, you must not hit it too hard. Therefore, you should relax your hand somewhat to cushion the shot. Your forward movement at impact will supply most of the power you need.

The racket's path is slightly down and through the ball (as shown in Figure 13), as opposed to chopping the ball with a severe downward movement.

On the volley, the racket head should be held above the wrist, and the stroke made with a forward movement of the arm and wrist and a small shoulder turn. You will need the shoulder turn more on the backhand than the forehand because your arm and wrist are weaker on the backhand, particularly if you use a two-handed backhand (see Figure 14).

The proper grip for the volley is the Continental grip for both the forehand and backhand. This grip is basically half-way between the Eastern forehand and backhand grips (it's also the same grip used on the serve). Although some good volleyers have switched grips, using their normal forehand

1

2

3

FIGURE 13.
Forehand volley.

FIGURE 14.
Backhand volley.

1

2

3

THINK TO WIN

and backhand ground stroke grips, the majority of players use the Continental. This grip will produce a slightly open racket face and facilitate the chipping motion of both strokes. You will also be able to switch between backhand and forehand volleys without changing grips. There often is simply not enough time to switch grips during rapid exchanges.

The final crucial factor in the volleyer is your eyes. Obviously you should watch the ball closely on all strokes, but the volley is less forgiving on mishits. With a ground stroke you generally clear the net by several feet and do not aim close to the lines. With a volley, however, you usually play within inches of the net and closer to the lines. (You cannot afford simply to plop the ball in the middle of the court. When you come to the net, you must put the ball away within a shot or two or you are likely to be passed.) Because the margin for error on the volley is so thin, a mishit at the net usually costs you the point. On the baseline, by contrast, a mishit may reduce your net clearance or allow your opponent to attack you, but it generally will not be immediately fatal.

Compounding the problem is that mishits are more likely at the net than at the baseline. The ball is moving faster (since it hasn't bounced and slowed down) and travels a shorter distance, so you have less time to see it. And because you usually are moving during the volley, the ball becomes even harder to track. Therefore it pays to make a special effort to watch the ball all the way to the racket on the volley.

More players are sound ground strokers than sound volleyers. It is not necessarily that they have more aptitude for the ground stroke; it is because they do not practice the volley correctly. In order to master any physical skill, you must practice it exactly as it is intended to be used. For example, in playing the piano, a pianist must repeatedly strike the proper notes in sequence to learn a particular song. Eventually through muscle memory, his fingers will seek out the exact pattern that he has rehearsed without conscious effort or thought. If he practices the wrong sequence of notes, this improper sequence will come out at

. . . .

FIGURE 15.
One step volley.

1

2

the recital. Obviously he can't practice one way and expect to play a different way when it counts.

But most tennis players do this all the time when they practice their volley. Under match conditions, volleys are hit while moving, integrating the eyes, hands, and legs in the stroke. Yet, like a pianist practicing an improper sequence of notes, most players practice the volley while standing still or taking just one mechanical step (see Figure 15).

They wind up practicing a shot that they should not hit in a match. Ground strokes are different. With ground strokes, practice and match conditions are much the same. Since the object is to reach the ball early, stop, set up, and hit, the player will generally practice this sequence exactly as he would do it in a match. But volleyers rarely practice as they play.

What's wrong with practicing the volley this way? Because when a player hits a moving volley, he gets much of his power from his legs. He is forced to learn a short swing because a long one will give him too much power and he'll lose control of the shot. By practicing the volley standing still, a player gets into the habit of using a longer stroke because he needs it to generate enough power. Then in a match, when he uses the swing that he learned in practice, he must either stop to hit it, or keep moving and lose control of his volleys.

This is why coaches are always screaming at their pupils to shorten their swings on their volleys. But when you volley standing still, a long swing comes naturally. Where else can you get the power you need? Getting players to give up this habit, once it is ingrained, is as difficult as getting an incumbent out of office. But if they would practice moving as they hit the volley, the problem would disappear. (Unfortunately, the incumbent problem would remain.)

Furthermore, a player moving through the volley must learn to follow and react to a faster-moving ball. That's because the ball's closing velocity is, in fact, the ball's velocity plus his own velocity as he moves forward. A volleyer who stands still, on the other hand, sees a slower ball and he becomes accustomed to having the extra time. Under match conditions, a player who practices standing volleys will hesitate at moving forward because to do so would create a novel and uncomfortable situation in which the action is speeded up. If he tries to stand still to get a better look, he will have to contact the ball too far from the net. If he tries to run through the volley, he is likely to miss. No wonder he has problems!

It was once thought that ground strokers could be made, but you had to be born a volleyer. This was true only because ground strokers practiced the same strokes they used in matches, while volleyers practiced strokes they didn't use (or, at least, shouldn't use). If they tried to learn to volley that way, they had *better* be born volleyers. But *any* physical habit can be learned with enough proper practice.

My team at Pepperdine spends a great deal of time on volley drills. The volleyer starts a foot or two behind the service line. When the ball is fed to him, he accelerates forward as far as possible before striking the ball. His opponent on the baseline is instructed to mix lobs in with ground strokes so that whenever the volleyer moves in too close to the net, the lob goes over his head. The volleyer learns to be constantly wary of the lob, and to cover the net area in the forward-backward directions as well as laterally.

If the volleyer hits the ball in the area between the safe position and the net (see Diagram 14), he must put on the brakes and back up to the safe position before his opponent hits the next shot.

The safe position is the closest distance to the net wherein the volleyer can still cover a lob over his head. It is generally located slightly behind the midpoint between the service line and the net, but it varies according to the situation and the player's physical ability. For example, if you approach the net behind a ball you hit extremely deep, you can move in closer to the net. Or if you are particularly quick and a good jumper, you can afford to get slightly closer than normal. Your safe position also depends on how clever a lobber your opponent is. If he telegraphs the shot and you can see the lob coming early, you can shade your

Diagram 14

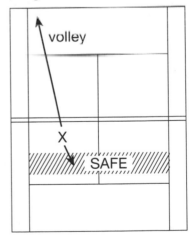

1   2   3

FIGURE 16.
FIGURE 16.
Moving on the volley.

position forward. With experience you will learn exactly what position is safe for you in any given situation.

In the instant before his opponent strikes the ball, the volleyer must pause wherever he is in the court. Then if it is a lob, the volleyer backs up; if it is a drive, he accelerates forward to volley. He is constantly trying to recognize as early as possible whether his opponent will lob or drive. Then he constantly moves backward and forward as the situation dictates.

The volleyer's movement is two-dimensional. He must move forward and back—in on the volley and back toward the safe position after he hits. And he also must move laterally to stay on the same side of the court as the ball. A baseliner, on the other hand, needs to move in only one dimension, recovering back to the center of the court when pulled wide.

To move forward, a volleyer ideally should take several small steps rather than one large one. This gives you better balance by keeping your legs under you. It allows you to move to the next shot more quickly. Notice in Figure 16 that the volleyer's legs end up parallel to the net in the

4   5   6

course of the shot. This allows him to move easily in any direction afterward.

If you take one long step on your forehand volley (see Figure 15), you end up having to take an extra step in order to move to the next ball. This is because you must bring your legs up parallel to the net before you can move to your left.

Being able to lunge or jump for passing shots is a valuable skill which all volleyers should develop. When your opponent whacks a wide passing shot and there is no time to run to the ball, you can, as a last resort, cover the most ground by jumping. Yannick Noah, John McEnroe, and Boris Becker can, when pressed, reach nearly halfway across the court with a single leap. They actually hit the ball with both feet off the ground, diving through the air. The stroke itself relies on a powerful wrist snap, since they contact the ball at the extreme end of their reach. Though these superb athletes usually return to earth upright, Becker has entertained audiences with some spectacular crash landings.

To improve this skill (jumping, not crash-landing), the

volleyer should practice jumping for any shot that appears out of reach, even if it is clearly too far away. In many cases you will surprise yourself by getting your racket on the ball. With time you will learn to control the volley while jumping and to cover shots that formerly looked unreachable.

Diving for the ball takes split-second timing. You usually have to do it when your volley falls short in the court and gives your opponent a passing shot on which he can stop, set up, and tee off. You should not simply pick a side, wait until the last instant, and run to it. Instead you can make one of two possible plays.

The first is to position yourself at the safe position on the same side of the court as the ball. Your primary responsibility is to guard against the down-the-line passing shot because it will get by you the fastest. Now you have the sideline and the middle of the court covered, but your opponent can still get the ball past you with a perfect, sharp-angled crosscourt. You have to concede him this shot. If he hits it, he is just too good. But don't try to cover the whole court, because it can't be done. The crosscourt passing shot must travel farther to get by you, so you have slightly more time to reach it. That is why you leave a little more room for your opponent to hit the passing shot there.

Then lower your center of gravity by crouching down to prepare to spring with your legs and, with your eyes open extra wide, watch the baseliner like a hawk. As he begins his stroke, you will start to get a sense of where he will hit the ball, and you should drift or lean in that direction, though never committing totally. Continually watch the baseliner closely and be prepared to change direction at the last instant, if necessary. Then, as the ball is hit, leap for it.

The second play is to try to sucker the baseliner into hitting his passing shot to a particular side. Purposely shade to one side, leaving a subtle unattended hole in your net coverage. Then, as his attention is occupied making the shot, drift toward the hole. If he has taken the bait, you should be able to cover the pass with a well-timed jump. In any case, you must keep your eyes glued to your opponent at all times during the development of his shot and be prepared to adjust your leap if he crosses you up.

In either case, the key to making the lunging volley in a split-second reaction situation is to remain relaxed and flexible. And you should make a conscious effort to relax because you will have a natural tendency to tense your muscles as you strain to anticipate the passing shot. Tense muscles lead to slower reactions and impair your ability to adjust to changes. As important as the point may be, and as determined as you may be to leap after any possible passing shot, you must resist the urge to make a "foot to the floorboard" type of maximal effort. Here, as in every situation at the net, you must stay loose, relaxed, and flexible.

Becoming a good volleyer takes time, effort, and proper practice. But a net attack is still the best way to put the ball away consistently. To sum up the key factors in hitting the volley:

1. Hit the volley while moving forward, coordinating the legs, hands, and eyes.
2. Anticipate the lob and distinguish early between your opponent's lob and drive.
3. Learn through practice to instinctively seek proper position at the net.
4. Develop the necessary mobility and balance by including a great deal of movement in your volley drills.

VOLLEY STRATEGY

The strategy at the net is, in many respects, exactly the opposite of baseline strategy. As we've seen, when in doubt on the baseline, the best place to hit the ball is crosscourt. At the net it is down-the-line. To understand why, look at Diagram 15, which shows you where a baseliner standing at position X might hit passing shots.

Once the ball reaches the crosshatched area, it has passed the volleyer. Distance A is the distance a passing shot travels down-the-line and distance B is the distance a passing shot travels crosscourt. Notice that distance A is shorter than distance B. This means the ball will take less time to pass the volleyer down-the-line than crosscourt. The volleyer cannot, therefore, stand in the center of the court for proper net coverage. His primary concern must be to cover the down-the-line passing shot because this shot gives him the least time to react. A down-the-line passing shot takes approximately 20 percent less time to get by the volleyer than does a crosscourt shot. The volleyer must then, as a general rule, stay on the same side of the court as the ball.

The safest place to hit the volley, therefore, is down-the-

Diagram 15

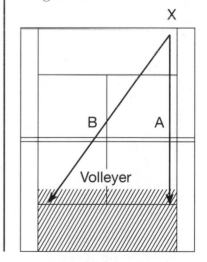

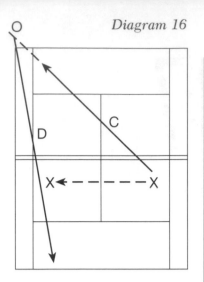

Diagram 16

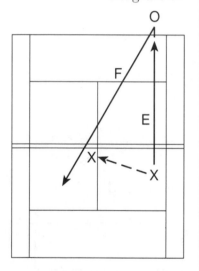

Diagram 17

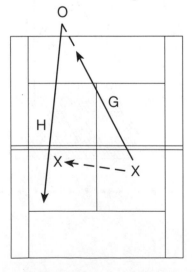

Diagram 18

line, because the volleyer will be in position to cover his opponent's next shot. If he hits the volley crosscourt, he must put the ball away or at least hurt his opponent severely, because the volleyer is momentarily out of position after hitting it. He must move quickly across the court in order to follow the ball and cover the opposite sideline. The wider crosscourt the net player hits his volley, the farther he must move to get into position for the next shot (see Diagram 16).

In Diagram 16 the volleyer hits wide crosscourt along pathway C and is exposed to a passing shot along pathway D. Unless his crosscourt volley is a winner or near-winner, it may be impossible for him to move fast enough to reach the down-the-line passing shot.

Let's say the volleyer faces a low ball and is not able to hit a winner or near-winner. In this situation, it is best to volley deep down-the-line so as to be in position for the next shot (see Diagram 17).

Here the volleyer is in proper net position after hitting the volley along pathway E. He is able to comfortably fulfill his primary responsibility of covering the line as well as lunge for a potential crosscourt pass along pathway F.

A second option for playing position on a passing shot that you can't put away is to volley *deep* crosscourt. Although the very best position play is to volley down the line, if you are not too far away from the center of the court this volley will usually allow you to cover your court (see Diagram 18).

Here the net player hits the volley along pathway G. That still allows him to reach the down-the-line pass along pathway H. He will have to move quickly to cover the open court, but not as quickly as if he had hit a wide crosscourt volley. Hitting the volley deep crosscourt may be a good percentage play if your opponent is weaker from that side of the court, for example, or a little slow. It may pay a mobile volleyer to give up a little position in order to reach an opponent's weaker side or make him run a greater distance.

As a general rule, the wide volley is the aggressive volley. You can often angle it far out of your opponent's reach, particularly if he tries to pass you down the line but doesn't hit the shot well enough. But beware of attempting to hit this shot prematurely. Players who are insecure at the net are often so panicked about being passed that they try to put away the first ball by hitting it into the open side of the court, no matter how difficult the shot may be. This is a case where it is well not to give your opponent too much credit. Passing shots are not easy to hit, particularly off of well-positioned deep balls. If you have a low, tough volley, relax and play it back deep. This will transfer the pressure back to your opponent.

The same logic holds for approach shots. All else being equal, the approach shot should be hit deep down-the-line. If you choose to approach crosscourt, the shot must hurt your opponent more to counterbalance the extra distance you must move to be in position for the volley. If you hit your approach wide crosscourt, it must be a winner or near-winner, since proper net coverage on the next shot will be virtually impossible. Again, if you are trying to attack your opponent's weaker side by hitting a crosscourt approach, it should be hit deep, not wide.

On either an approach or volley, if you are near the middle of the court you can hit to either side, since court coverage will not be greatly affected in any case. It is only when you are near one of the sidelines that position and court coverage become crucial issues in shot selection.

On the volley, as with ground strokes, depth is more important than power. At the tournament level, the deep volley should land within a foot or two of the baseline. If it lands shorter than that, a good ground stroker becomes dangerous because he can prepare early for the shot and lean his weight into the court as he hits. A truly deep volley, on the other hand, even if it is hit down the center of the court, makes the passing shot difficult.

The volleyer's general strategy is, therefore, fairly simple:

1. When you are at the net, protect against the down-the-line passing shot.
2. If you are near a sideline, volley down-the-line unless you can hit a winner or near-winner.

3. On balls that are low or otherwise difficult to handle, relax and volley deep.
4. Depth is more important than power.

THE WAR BETWEEN BASELINERS AND VOLLEYERS

A classic confrontation in tennis occurs when a baseliner faces a volleyer in a match. It's interesting to watch the clash of diametrically opposite styles, to see how the inherent advantages and disadvantages of both strategies come into play during the match. But there's more going on than a mere clash of styles. The war between baseliners and volleyers often turns on the psychological battles that are also being waged.

The mental game is so important because both strategies rely on putting pressure on your opponent. The fact is that it is very difficult for volleyers to win each point by putting the ball away. It's equally, if not more difficult for baseliners to hit clean passing shots every time their opponent ventures to the net. Tennis is a game of errors. Winning—whether you are a baseliner or a volleyer—ultimately depends on including your opponent to help you by making mistakes. The successful baseliner hits some clean passing shots but wins a crucial number of additional points by threatening his opponent into missing approach shots and volleys. The winning volleyer, on the other hand, puts away some volleys but eventually succeeds by scaring his opponent into overplaying and missing passing shots.

That's why a volleyer must beware of giving his opponent too much credit for his ability to hit passing shots. You do not have to put away every volley you get your racket on. Some can, of course, be hit for immediate winners. But many cannot, and must be played for position. Here you must have confidence in your ability to move at the net and reach the next ball.

Volleys hit from below the level of the net are generally hard to put away. You should almost invariably play these back deep. The novice or panicky volleyer will force the winner by trying to angle the ball off, hit it too hard, or attempt to drop volley. He will succeed only in making too many errors or exposing himself to the easy pass. The good volleyer relaxes, goes for depth, and looks for a better opportunity for the winner. Do not let fear of the passing shot dictate shot selection.

In the war against the baseliners the persistent volleyer has several inherent advantages—not insurmountable advantages, but advantages nonetheless. First of all, passing shots are easier to hit at the beginning of a match than they are at the end. The baseliner is under pressure with a man at the net and this mounts over time. It is emotionally wearing to have a hit passing shot after passing shot. Sometimes it seems as if baseliners have only so many passing shots in them and eventually simply run out.

Another problem for the baseliner is that proper execution of the passing shot requires the ball to be hit hard, close to the line, and deceptively. This takes great precision, and the baseliner must be at the proper emotional level to do it consistently. He must be up, excited—but not too excited. Diagram 19 shows the inverted U-shaped curve which represents the relationship between excitement (tension level) and success with the passing shot (performance).

As you can see, if the baseliner is either too relaxed or too tense, he won't pass well. Somewhere between these extremes lies the optimum performance level.

Early in the match a baseliner is normally playing at a relatively low tension level. His opponent's approach to the

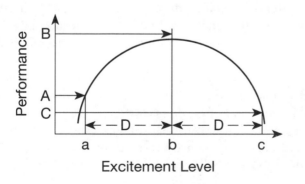

Diagram 19

net naturally raises the tension level somewhat and he may pass quite well. Passing shots are not hard to hit at 2-all in the first set. But late in the third set, when the outcome of the match hinges on a few points, the tension level is already high—near the breaking point, in fact. Any increase in tension level can push the baseliner over the brink and cause a marked decrease in performance. Passing shots—even easy ones—are very difficult to hit at 6-all in the third set tiebreaker. You can see this displayed graphically by reviewing Diagram 19.

In Diagram 19, the tension level early in the match is assumed to be at point a. An opponent advancing to the net raises it by an amount D to tension level b. This helps the baseliner to perform at the correspondingly high performance level B. He is likely, therefore, to hit his passing shot well. But let us assume that late in the match the tension level is at point b. A net attack would again raise this by an amount D to tension level c, but now this would cause the baseliner to perform at the correspondingly low performance level C. And he would probably miss the passing shot.

Adding to the baseliner's woes is the fact that somewhere along the line he will miss an easy passing shot or two—sitters where the ball lands short in the center of the court and begs to be knocked off. It may not happen right away, but if anyone is forced to pass repeatedly, the human error factor will eventually surface. Hitting close to the line requires a near-perfect stroke and no one can be that perfect all the time. Once the baseliner muffs the easy passing shot, he knows he is capable of missing *any* passing shot. No matter how many great shots he makes thereafter, doubt now lurks in his mind. It can surface late in the match when the pressure is intense and cause further easy errors.

That's not to say that a baseline strategy is doomed against someone who continually comes to the net. A skilled baseliner can and often does beat a persistent volleyer. He too has certain inherent advantages. Among them is the fact that most players are more adept at the baseline than at the net. Great volleyers are rare, so passing shots need

THINK TO WIN

not be aimed for the outside edge of the line. The most important thing is that passing shots be hit in the court *all the time*. The volleyer must then hit four put-aways to win a game—and that is difficult. The volleyer depends on the baseliner missing a healthy percentage of passing shots. You can make his life miserable by not obliging.

The secret to hitting passing shots is to consciously make an effort to relax during the stroke. This counteracts the natural tendency to tighten up and press too hard to keep the ball away from the volleyer. Never give the volleyer too much credit for greatness. Just relax, watch the ball, pick a side, and smoothly go for your shot. Never watch the volleyer. The ball is moving much faster than he is and requires your complete attention. You learn to anticipate the volleyer's position and moves through experience.

Use some topspin on all passing shots if you can. A topspin shot is better than any other kind of stroke because it can be hit hard and still the ball will dip down into the court after crossing the net. The descending ball will be difficult to volley even if the net player reaches it. If you can't hit topspin, use a flat stroke to pass. Slice (underspin) is the least useful stroke for passing, because its tendency to float will not allow you to hit the ball hard and keep it in the court.

When in doubt, the best place to direct your passing shot is crosscourt, over the low part of the net (see Diagram 20).

A passing shot hit along pathway E does not allow the volleyer to get a sharp angle on a putaway volley (pathway F). If the passing shot is not hit too high, a quick baseliner can usually run the volley down.

The down-the-line pass is more risky. Although you can get the ball past a volleyer more quickly down-the-line and have more depth of court into which you can hit (a crosscourt pass must be angled rather sharply into very little court area to pass cleanly), a down-the-line pass *must* be hit for a winner. If the net player reaches the ball, it is relatively easy for him to angle off the next volley for a winner (see Diagram 21).

These rules on the passing shot apply only when there is no clear-cut opening. The baseliner and volleyer are play-

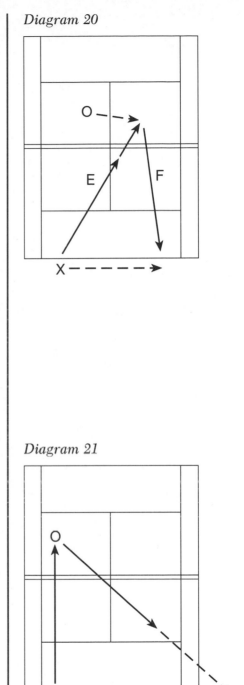

Diagram 20

Diagram 21

ing a guessing game and you should hit the passing shot wherever you sense that there is a good opening, whether it's crosscourt or down-the-line.

But even the best baseliner shouldn't just park himself permanently in the backcourt. It is advantageous for anyone, no matter how poorly he may volley, to advance to the net on certain balls. The cardinal rule on approach shots is that *the worse one volleys or the better one's opponent passes, the better the approach shot must be.* If one volleys horribly, the approach must be a near-winner to ensure a sufficiently easy volley. If one volleys well, the approach can be ordinary or even poor. The volleyer's ability at the net will make up the difference. However, if the opponent passes well, obviously the approach shot must be stronger.

Early in the match a player should decide how short in the court or high his opponent's shot should be in order to elicit an approach and volley. The poor volleyer will need a very short, high ball (well inside the service line), while the excellent volleyer can come in on balls that land somewhat deeper than the service line. If the volleyer finds he is being consistently passed, the approach will have to be made off shorter balls. If the volleyer is winning an exceptionally high percentage of points, he can start coming in sooner off deeper balls. But once you have decided on what type of ball is good for your net attack, stick to your approach criteria as long as the percentages are in your favor. Do not change your criteria because of the score. As long as the percentages are better than fifty-fifty, approaches and volleys should be made to pay over and over like a slot machine.

SERVE

8

The serve is the most complex and difficult of all strokes to learn. The racket travels the greatest distance and moves at the highest velocity. It also contains the largest number of separate elements which must be combined and put in proper sequence with exact timing. As most teaching pros discover, once a player learns an improper technique, straightening it out becomes extremely difficult.

Serving has much in common with various types of overhand throwing motions, such as pitching a baseball or tossing the javelin. The hand is accelerated by using the legs, trunk, shoulders, arm, and wrist in a linked chain reaction. Ultimately you achieve maximum hand velocity (hence, racket velocity) by adding the components of velocity contributed by (1) throwing the body up and forward with the legs and torso, (2) accelerating the arm by rotating the shoulders, and (3) snapping the wrist.

When you move your arm by rotating your shoulders, you are only accelerating your arm in the horizontal plane. But since your serve is an overhand motion, you must accelerate your racket vertically at the same time. Straight

1   2   3   4

FIGURE 17.
Service action.

ening your bent legs and snapping your torso forward throw your arm up and over your head. If you do not do this, you would have to rely entirely on your shoulder muscles to move your arm up.

Notice in frames 4, 5, and 6 of Figure 17 how the legs and torso are used to drive the body upward and forward.

A comfortable stance for the server is sideways to the direction of the hit. If an imaginary line is drawn connecting the toes of each foot, it would point in the direction you are going to serve. (John McEnroe uses a completely different position, which we will discuss later.) As you toss the ball up, you bend your knees and torso and draw your right leg forward (see Figure 17). As the ball reaches the top of its arc, you start your power action by straightening your knees and torso to drive your body upward and in the direction of the court. Most pros actually launch themselves into the air with the force of their leg drive. They are not deliberately jumping, however. Their momentum simply carries them off the ground.

As you complete the power action, your weight falls forward into the court, and you catch it with your right leg (if you are right-handed). Though it looks like a step, it really isn't. If the server simply steps into the court, it ruins the

5   6   7   8

serving sequence by turning the shoulders forward too soon (see Figure 18).

There are many players who catch the forward thrust of their weight on their left leg rather than the right (see Figure 19).

There have been many inconclusive arguments about whether it is better to land on your right or your left leg. The great servers of the past appear about equally divided.

9

1   2

FIGURE 18.
Serving improperly
by stepping too soon.

1   2   3   4

FIGURE 19.
Server landing on his left leg.

Many of the older ones, like Pancho Gonzales, Stan Smith, and John Newcombe, preferred their right legs, but greats like Arthur Ashe, Ivan Lendl, Stefan Edberg, and John McEnroe (if he were serving right-handed) landed on their left legs. It is a tough call, but if a player were following his serve to the net consistently, it seems better to me to land on your right leg, as this sets you running forward and on balance immediately.

Another element coming into play at the beginning of the power action is shoulder rotation. Referring to frames 2, 3, and 4 of Figure 17, we can see how the shoulders rotate about twenty to thirty degrees away from the target as the ball is tossed up. This makes the shoulders act like a coiled spring to generate power.

As the power action begins, the shoulders are rotated forward violently, flinging the arm out from behind the neck by centrifugal force. The shoulders should rotate in excess of 120 degrees. During this process the arm must be relaxed. A loose, passive arm creates no resistance as the shoulders throw it forward. If you actively use your arm muscles during the serve, you only slow down your serve. Essentially, the arm is snapped out from behind the neck like a bullwhip by shoulder rotation as well as straightening the legs and torso.

5   6   7

In Figure 20, you can see how shoulder rotation is used to accelerate the arm when throwing a ball.

Like winding a spring, the shoulders are coiled away from the target. As the action begins, the shoulders are uncoiled by rotating forward, accelerating the ball. (In fact, the same basic motion is used for throwing the javelin as well as for most other throwing activities.)

A novice at throwing a ball does not use any shoulder

FIGURE 20.
Throwing a ball.

1   2   3   4

FIGURE 21.
Throwing a ball improperly.

1

2

3

FIGURE 22.
The John McEnroe serve.

1

2

rotation and faces the target when he throws (see Figure 21). Since the throw begins with the person facing forward, it is analogous to a spring which is already sprung. No power now can come from shoulder rotation. It must be generated solely by the arm muscles.

According to John Yandell, who is a renowned analyst and has done extensive video work with John McEnroe, McEnroe differs from most servers in that he uses an extreme amount of shoulder rotation. He starts by standing with his back facing the net, employing almost 180 degrees of shoulder rotation (compared with just more than 120 degrees for most players; see Figure 22).

Notice how his feet are placed parallel along the baseline rather than in line with his target. Only one leg is now available to provide forward leg drive; if he used both, he

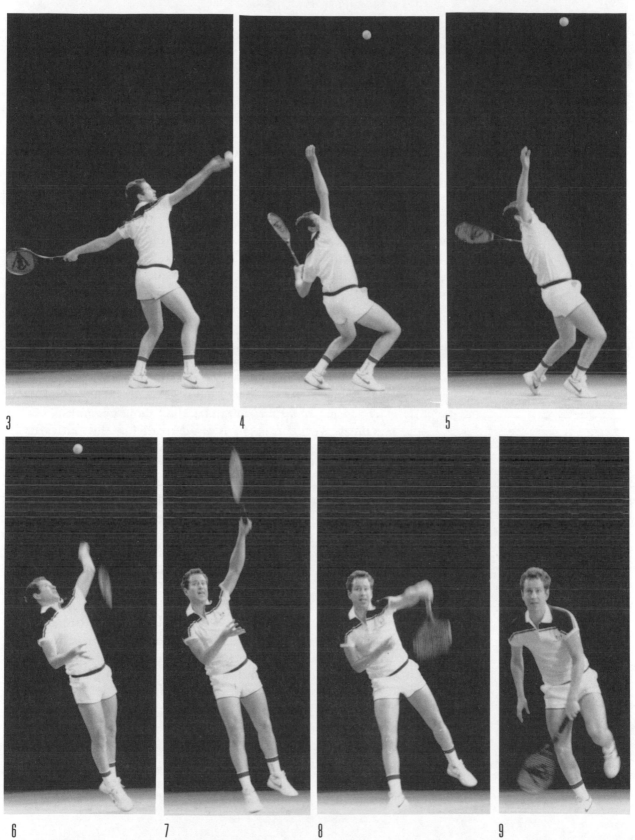

3

4

5

6

7

8

9

would be driven in a direction perpendicular to the direction of his serve. McEnroe has traded off one leg's drive to gain an additional sixty degrees of shoulder rotation. Since shoulder rotation is probably the most potent source of power in the serve, McEnroe has probably made a good trade and increased the velocity of his serve. However, there is no free lunch. I also suspect it is more difficult to control the direction of your serve with McEnroe's motion. McEnroe can serve as well as he does because he is a genius. Most ordinary mortals are probably best off leaving his technique alone.

The final element in generating power on the serve is the wrist snap. This occurs after the racket has been flung out from behind the neck by the shoulders, legs, and torso. The wrist is the final accelerator and simply adds its velocity to those already provided by the other sources. The beginning server should consciously begin the power action by rotating his shoulders and then, *after* the racket has been thrown forward in front of his shoulder, snap his wrist. The action of the wrist snap is shown in Figure 23. (You can also see the wrist used in Figure 21 in throwing a ball.)

The term *pronation* is often bandied about when discussing the serve. This term is used to define the outward rotation of the forearm as the wrist is snapped. To visualize the action of pronation, imagine reaching over your head to unscrew a light bulb with your right hand. The counterclockwise turn of the wrist and inward rotation of the forearm is precisely what happens in the serve after contact with the ball is made (see Figure 23).

Pronation is a descriptive term, but not a particularly useful one. A server need not consciously concern himself with trying to pronate when serving. The wrist and forearm will naturally pronate on your serve during the act of snapping your wrist. There is no need to tell a server to pronate, since there is really no other way it can physically be done. The server need only concentrate on snapping his wrist, making good contact, and directing the ball. Pronation will occur as an inexorable consequence.*

* As an aside, another example of pseudo-useful terminology in action is the talk about needing to use a scissor kick when you hit your overhead.

THINK TO WIN

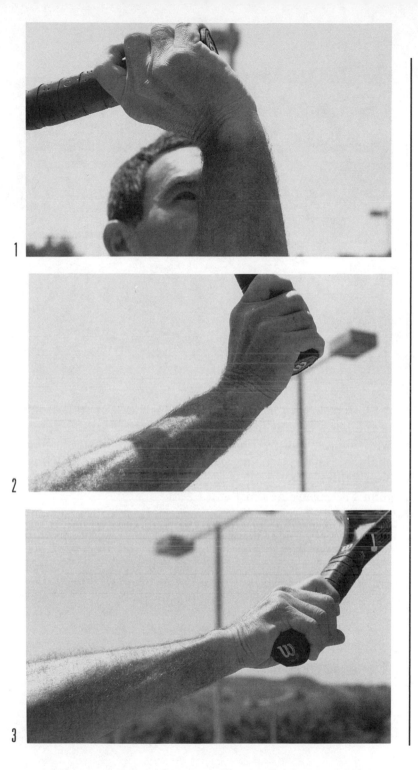

FIGURE 23.
Wrist action during serve.

1

2

3

FIGURE 24.
The frying-pan serve.

1   2

On the serve, the ball should be hit a foot or so in front of the body, and as high as the server can reach on tiptoe with his arm fully extended. The toss should peak at or slightly above this point. Most pros toss the ball slightly above the contact point and hit it on the way down (see John McEnroe's toss in Figure 22).

Only a few great servers—such as Roscoe Tanner and Kevin Curren—actually hit the ball at the peak of their toss. This requires perfect timing and coordination between the toss and racket swing. The racket must move a considerable distance and arrive at a particular point in time and space the exact instant the ball gets there. There is no

---

With a scissor kick, you jump up for your overhead off of your right leg (if you are right-handed) and, after completing the hit, land on your left leg, "scissoring" your legs in midair. If you try it yourself, you will soon see that this is the only way you can possibly do it. Trying to do it any other way will probably cause you to break your neck. And talking about how important it is to use a scissor kick on overheads and pronate when serving succeeds only in making the simple appear complicated.

3   4

leeway. On the other hand, a higher toss introduces some slack in the system. The server gains flexibility. He can slow down or speed up the action as the situation requires and contact the ball where he wants on its way down. His trade-off is having to hit a moving ball rather than a stationary one.

The best grip for the serve is the Continental grip. This grip allows you to hit both flat and spin serves without having to use unnatural wrist positions. Beginners usually like to use forehand grips or even an extreme Western grip (called a "pancake" grip because it looks like you're holding a frying pan). Those grips allow the serve to be hit with a very simple forward wrist movement (see Figure 24).

Parenthetically, beginners often serve with their shoulders facing forward as shown in Figure 24. This forces them to generate most of their racket velocity by using their arm and shoulder muscles, much like the novices do when throwing a ball (see Figure 21). They do this because they can control the racket better this way. As with the improperly hit (pushed) backhand, they get constant feedback

· ·

from proprioceptive nerves in their muscles. These nerves tell them the exact position of their arm and racket at any instant, so they can control the serve immediately. Unfortunately, they can never generate very high racket velocity this way.

The Continental grip feels very awkward on the serve at first. In fact, on the first few tries it usually causes you to serve directly into the side fence. It is also unnerving because the racket head approaches the ball on edge. The novice can't believe that the strings will actually contact the ball that way. Of course, the natural pronation of the wrist and forearm ultimately expose the strings to the ball at contact. With practice, however, a player learns to control the direction of the ball with the wrist. With time, a variety of flat and spin serves can be learned. It is very difficult to hit spin serves with a forehand grip, and spin is a valuable weapon on first serves and an absolute essential on all good second serves.

Conceptually, the problem on the second serve is how to hit it easy enough to get it in consistently yet hard enough not to be a duck for your opponent. Spin, of course, is the answer. With a spin serve, you impart a tremendous amount of energy to the ball, but not in the form of velocity. So you store energy in the ball in the form of spin while it travels through the air at a relatively low velocity. But when it hits the court, its spin energy is released. The ball grabs and accelerates, making the return difficult.

Spin also gives you an extra margin of safety to clear the net and still get the ball into the court. The more spin (especially topspin) you have on your second serve, the better. To put topspin on your second serve, toss the ball farther behind you and more over your head than on a first serve. As you start the power action, concentrate on hitting up on the ball by driving up with your legs and violently snapping your wrist.

Most advanced players swing as hard, or harder, on the second serve as on the first. The ball moves through the air slower because so much of the energy goes into the spin, but the swing itself is harder. In fact most good servers swing as hard as they can on the second serve. The more spin the server can impart to the ball, the safer the serve becomes.

Many recreational players make the mistake of trying to hit their flat first serves as hard as they can. It is better to relax and use somewhere between 85 and 95 percent of your maximum power. It will make surprisingly little difference in the resulting power of your serve. Pushing it to the limit usually decreases coordination and timing enough to nullify any increase in raw power. All that results is a substantial increase in errors and maybe a sore arm.

Your goal is to get approximately two-thirds (67 percent) of your first serves in the court (50 percent might be the lower limit). Too many faults on first serves leaves you vulnerable to double faults and—less obvious but equally important—starting out too many points on the defensive. Most players are not prepared to attack your first serve, even if it is weak. But they will move forward like vultures on the second. They know you must get the second serve in and cannot afford to take excessive chances. With the first serve you have the leeway to choose a stronger delivery, and that uncertainty keeps your opponents off balance. So monitor your first-serve percentage during a match.

Of course, everyone would like to get more first serves in the court. But in a match there is not enough time to get out with your pro during the changeovers and practice serving a bucket of balls. However, you can improve your percentage without practice by simply serving easier. Most players mistakenly allow power to determine first-serve percentage rather than the other way around. They pick an arbitrarily high level of power and bang away without regard to the percentage that go in. The proper way is to decide on how frequently you want to get your first serve in and determine your power accordingly.

Once the mechanics of the serve are mastered, the server should focus on a few basics in preparation for each delivery. The most important is to relax, particularly the arm and wrist. Some servers even shake their arm around as they move into the ready position in order to loosen it up. They know a stiff arm cannot be whipped forward as fast and that the snapping action of the wrist will be hindered.

A second thing to concentrate on is the ball toss and extending upward fully on the serve. An improper ball toss is a major reason many players have trouble with their serves. I see servers perfectly willing to chase errant tosses all over the sky rather than taking more care with the toss itself. Visualize where you want to make contact with the ball and then carefully toss the ball to that spot. The server should also visualize reaching up very high and snapping his wrist down on a high ball.

During match play, you can usually correct most errors by adjusting the toss and wrist snap. If the previous serve went into the net, try to contact the ball slightly higher. This will make it land deeper in the court. A small increase in the height of your contact point (about one-half to one inch) is usually enough. If the previous serve went long, focus on snapping your wrist slightly earlier in the serving sequence. This will tend to drive the ball down shorter in the court. In making adjustments, however, be aware that there is a direct relationship between the toss and wrist snap. If the server reacts to a netted serve by raising the contact point, the next serve will probably go long unless he also snaps his wrist sooner at the same time.

Notice in the previous discussion I used the terminology *raising the contact point* rather than *tossing the ball higher*. These are often two very different things. Many players react to a low contact point by simply throwing the ball up higher. Then they slow down their swing, wait for the ball to drop, and hit it at the usual low altitude. The focus must be consciously on contact point rather than the height of the toss. This allows the racket to come through in time to meet the ball before it drops too low.

LOB

The lob is a much-maligned, underused, and little-understood stroke. But if you like winning tennis matches, it is probably the best friend you have. Most people at the recreational level do not possess reliable enough overheads to overpower a determined lobber. They depend on the baseliner's macho instincts to tempt him to try difficult passing shots from bad positions rather than throw up high lobs and test their overheads (and nerves).

If an opponent does not have a consistently reliable overhead, I would go to the lob as my *first* line of defense against a net attack. When in doubt, lob! I would pass only on easy balls or after I had driven my opponent a few feet back from his normal net position with lobs. Even at the tournament level, the lob should be mixed in and used as an equal partner with the passing shots in defense against the volleyer. An opponent venturing to the net should be equally wary of your three options: the down-the-line passing shot, the crosscourt passing shot, and the lob. This makes his odds of guessing correctly one in three rather than fifty-fifty (as they would be if he only had passing shots to worry about). Moreover, the threat of the lob forces him to play back from the net, making it easier for you to pass him *and* more difficult for him to put away the volley even if he gets to it.

There are two basic varieties of lob—offensive and defensive—which are used in totally different situations. The *offensive* lob is designed to get over the volleyer's head and send him scurrying back to the baseline in a vain or, at least, awkward attempt to chase the ball down. It is hit rather low and the ball must move relatively quickly through the air in order to get over the net man and down into the court before he knows what happened. Deception is crucial.

A *defensive* lob, on the other hand, is not really intended to get over the volleyer's head. It is just designed to offer him a difficult target. The defensive lob should be hit as high as possible. The greater the altitude, the faster the ball will be traveling as it returns to earth—hence, the more difficult it is to time the overhead. Ideally, your lob will have gone so high the attacker will not dare to hit it on the fly. Rather, he will be forced to play the overhead after the ball has bounced (hopefully, somewhere near the baseline), and this will give you ample time to recover good court position and anticipate the direction of the smash.

The high defensive lob, when hit persistently and well, can really take all the fun out of coming to the net. Picture yourself hitting a great approach which sends your opponent scrambling, off balance, into the corner. Only a perfect passing shot can beat you. Anything less gives you an easy volley winner into an open court. Since the odds on his hitting the perfect pass are about one in twenty, you momentarily feel good that your risky approach, played so hard and close to the line, has paid off. Or has it? Instead of manfully attempting the hopeless pass from the vicinity of the side fence, your cowardly opponent lobs the ball into the cumulonimbus of a passing frontal system. Cursing, you wait, watch, and worry. Having already used up most of your allotment of good fortune making the tough approach shot, you wisely let the ball bounce, and, with a sigh of resignation, start the point over. Your opponent has got-

1   2   3   4

FIGURE 25. Forehand lob.

ten the good deal. You have risked the difficult approach shot and he's gotten even with an easy lob.

Like any other ground stroke, you should hit the lob in a precise and consistent manner. Players have a tendency to just poke the ball skyward with a makeshift stroke. They assume that since there is a lot of space up in the air, pinpoint accuracy is not really necessary. Or they try to be particularly cunning and deceptive by holding the shot until the last instant and jabbing at the ball. Sometimes they are just scrambling off balance and don't feel there is time to prepare a normal stroke. But in every case you would be better off with a sound mechanical stroke.

The basic lob should have a short backswing and long follow-through as shown in Figure 25. Note the shoulders are turned and prepared early, as with any other ground stroke, and the follow-through is of normal length. As with most other strokes, the shoulder turn provides the basic source of power. What distinguishes the lob from the drive (in addition to its very high follow-through), is its short backswing. This is necessary because the lob is a "touch" rather than "power" shot. Because of its trajectory, normal drive power will propel your lob into the fence rather than the court, so the racket must move rather slowly at impact.

5

Since the *only* purpose of the long backswing is to allow room for the racket to accelerate up to high speed, there is no need for a long backswing on a lob. A short backswing allows you to keep your power under control while maintaining a normal full follow-through.

Many players, however, insist on taking a normal long backswing on lobs. Now, in order to keep power under control, they are forced into one of two unattractive options. The first is to swing the racket very slowly and carefully throughout its long journey forward. This not only makes the shot difficult to control, but generously gives their opponents ample warning that a lob is on the way. The second alternative is to swing normally until the racket approaches the point of contact, and there abruptly slow it down so that it's not traveling too fast at impact. This, of course, produces a short follow-through, but is necessary so that the ball will remain in the county where the tennis match is being held. The problem here is that the jerky racket deceleration and abbreviated follow-through make the stroke imprecise. By contrast, lobbing with a short backswing and normal long follow-through allow great accuracy and consistency. And the stroke must, obviously, start low and end high (see Figure 25).

Since the lob is a touch shot (like a drop shot), the wrist should be kept relaxed and flexible, which increases control and allows for last-minute adjustments. The pros term this "soft hands," but it really refers to suppleness or "give" in the wrist at impact. It also helps keep the ball from traveling too far. When a player becomes tense and tries to lob with an inflexible, stiff wrist (known in the business as "rock hands"), the ball ricochets off the racket and heads for the far reaches of the arena.

The basic lob is struck flat and can be used either for offense or defense. The difference is in its trajectory. Defensive lobs are aimed more vertically and hit harder (hence, higher). The offensive lob has a low trajectory, aiming to barely clear the net rusher's flailing racket.

The offensive lob should be used only when the baseliner is in control of the point. The best opportunity is when the volleyer's shot has landed short in the court and the lobber has the comfortable option of lobbing or passing. Here you can lean your weight into the court and the volleyer, sensing the passing shot, is likely to move forward. Because the backswing is so short, this type of lob is difficult to anticipate or read, and the ball gets over the volleyer's head before he knows what has hit him. If, on the other hand, the approach or volley has landed deep in the court, so that you are pushed backward and off balance, the volleyer will be expecting a lob. He will not be learning forward in anticipation of the pass, so fooling him with an offensive lob will be difficult. A high, defensive lob might be more in order here, since its success depends more on altitude than deception anyway.

There is another type of offensive lob which is totally different from the one I've just described. It is hit with heavy topspin and employs a full backswing, full follow-through, and terrific racket acceleration. The racket moves as fast as it does on the hardest ground stroke, and, in fact, the stroke looks very much like an ordinary topspin ground stroke. The difference is that the racket is drawn sharply upward, entailing greater use of the arm and wrist, and, of course, the trajectory of the ball is higher.

The topspin lob is extremely deceptive because the volleyer keys in on the speed of the racket coming forward and thinks he is going to see a passing shot. The volleyer frequently makes the fatal mistake of leaning forward as the ball is struck. The ball moves so swiftly through the air that once it gets over the volleyer's head, he has little chance of running it down. And even if he manages to react in time to chase the ball, the extreme topspin on the ball makes it accelerate away from him after the bounce.

The topspin lob is a two-edged sword. It is a very difficult shot to execute, but, if hit properly, it's a devastating weapon. It is particularly treacherous to play off of balls which have landed deep in the court and are rising at impact. On the other hand, if hit properly, it will generally succeed with disastrous effect on any foolhardy volleyer who is crowding the net. The psychological effect is a pleasant bonus for the baseliner. The net man is made insecure and forced to play back from the net—weakening the effectiveness of his volley and opening him up for the passing shot. But a poorly hit topspin lob is a sitting duck for the net player. I would warn all but the most advanced players to confine their interests in this shot to watching it on television.

Both offensive and defensive lobs are essential weapons in any player's repertoire, regardless of his level of play or the effectiveness of his opponent's overhead. Even when facing a net rusher with a great overhead, you must hit some offensive lobs to keep him honest. Once a volleyer figures out that you are going to rely exclusively on passing shots, he will "cheat" forward and crowd the net. This allows him to reach and put away passing shots more easily. So even if you have to sacrifice a few points early on to overhead winners, you should throw in a few offensive lobs to pin the volleyer back and set him up for the pass. Gauge the percentages. If you are up against a good jumper with a strong overhead and you judge he is most likely to put away overheads, use your lob early in the match on unimportant points to set him up for your passing shot later, in the crucial situation. If the reverse is the case, hold the lob in reserve and surprise him with it when you need the point.

A defensive lob is the shot of choice when you are in so much trouble that your winning passing shot percentage is low. The highest percentage chance you have of winning the point may be to force your opponent to hit an overhead off the bounce, deep in the court. But even if you lose the point, the lob will still pay dividends by keeping your opponent under constant pressure. A player who is penuriously denied free points, even after he has hit his best approach shot or volley, and must painfully earn each point by hitting overheads off of high lobs, is a player likely to make mistakes late in the match. Like the Chinese water torture, the negative effect of persistent lobbing is cumulative and debilitating. Bombardment with high lobs eventually tempts a player to overplay approach shots and volleys in an effort to end the agony.

SPECIAL-PURPOSE STROKES | 10

10

SERVE RETURN

Say you are up against a heavy hitter with a thunderous serve and it is an important point. What are your options?

1. Jump around and make noise in order to distract him during his motion.
2. Take a good swing and hope for the best.
3. Just try to poke the ball back anywhere in the court.
4. Pray for a double fault.
5. Develop a serve return which can nullify his delivery.

Whether we are willing to admit it or not, most of us have done all of these things at one time or another. On the other hand, everyone would like to develop a return of serve that can counterstrike even the biggest servers. Here are some considerations that can help you do just that.

Returning serve requires you to overcome two obstacles. The first is figuring out where the ball is going and the second is getting control of the fast-moving and/or fast-spinning ball. When facing a first serve, you must overcome both problems. When facing a second serve, you usually know where the ball is going, but you may have difficulty with its spin. Return techniques will therefore differ in the two cases.

Against a first serve, you must first decide where to stand. This involves what I call a "balance of hurt." There are two ways the server can hurt you. One is by the sheer speed of his serve. The ball may simply be moving so fast that you cannot react quickly enough to prepare and execute an effective stroke. The other way he can hurt you is with placement. The server may be able to aim the ball so accurately and with such disguise that you simply cannot reach it. You can neutralize each of these factors by standing in the proper position on the return. The problem is that each threat requires the exact opposite adjustment in position. It is impossible to stand in a position which simultaneously nullifies both threats. Thus, you are forced to compromise and pick a spot which balances the hurt so that no one of them becomes fatal.

To counter the speed of the serve, ideally you'd like to stand as deep in the court as possible. The increased distance between you and the server gives you extra time to react. On the other hand, if the server is able to hit either the centerline or the sideline without indication, your best counter is to stand in as close as possible to cut down his angles (see Diagram 22).

In Diagram 22 notice that a player standing close in at point A on the court has to traverse a distance *a* to reach the serve. Backing up to position B obliges you to traverse a longer distance *b* to reach the same serve. Thus, the farther back you stand, the farther you must move to cover wide serves. Of course, standing deep gives you more time to make this move, but because the ball travels a lot faster than you do, this will not be adequate compensation. If you stand deep, you are in jeopardy of being aced by well-directed serves.

Therefore, on high-velocity first serves, how deep you stand to return serve depends on the balance between how

Diagram 22

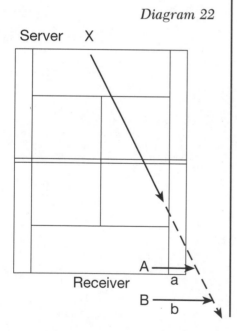

well your opponent can hit the corners of your service box and how fast he serves the ball. Ideally, you would like to stand near the back fence, but dare not because you will be aced by wide balls. So you move forward only as far as necessary to cover the wide serves. If your opponent is not good at hitting wide serves to both sides, you can stand quite far back. Otherwise you must come forward. And if he can serve with both high velocity *and* accuracy, you're in for a long afternoon.

Spin will usually be your problem when facing an opponent with an effective second serve. Your opponent will normally apply heavy topspin to the ball, and if the server is right-handed, the ball will either be sliced out to your right or kicked up and out to your left. In returning, your objective is to attack this serve, and to do so, you must contact the ball relatively close to your body. (A ball at the end of your reach is very difficult to control.) So you must position yourself as close in as possible.

Again you will be faced with the trade-off between speed and direction, but this time it's from a vantage point opposite from the first serve. Now the ball will be traveling relatively slowly through the air (otherwise the server is usually at too great a risk of a double fault), but the aggressive spin is likely to make the ball bounce up and away from you. Second serves by right-handers most commonly bounce up and out to a right-hander's backhand, and if you play too deep you will be constantly forced to hit high backhands at the limits of your reach. These are tough. But good lefty second serves are often even tougher, slicing out wider on your backhand side.

Standing in close nullifies this. You must, however, be prepared to make a few errors while becoming accustomed to the violence of the bounce. Sacrificing a few points or even a few games is a good trade for being able to hit returns close to your body for the rest of the match.

The real problems occur if your opponent not only can spin the second serve in well, but can also hit it consistently deep and with reasonable velocity. You will not be able to stand in as close as you might like because the ball will be upon you too quickly. What you must do, therefore, is note how often the speed of the ball catches you and move your stance back accordingly. A general rule is to stand in as close as the speed and depth of the second serve will let you.

The stroke itself for the return of serve should entail a short backswing. Serve returns, like everything else in tennis, involve compromise. The purpose of the backswing is power. The longer it is, the faster the racket can be moving at impact, but the more difficult it is to control. Since it is difficult to control a serve return to begin with, it is smart to trade some power for more control. Shorten the backswing. The ball will usually be moving rather fast on the serve anyway, so you will not need to add much additional energy to it with your racket.

Make a special effort to drive your weight forward into the shot. You are, of course, well advised to do this on any ground stroke, but here it becomes of greater importance than usual because you have sacrificed some of your normal power by taking an abbreviated backswing. You'll need a

FIGURE 26.
Forehand serve return.

1　　　　　2

　　　　　THINK TO WIN

little extra from your most controllable source of power—your legs. On a first serve, this may be difficult because you will often be forced to lunge out for the ball to one side or the other. But on second serves, you can almost always move forward.

Wait on or inside the baseline when returning a second serve and take a step forward as the server starts his toss. As he hits the serve, stay on the balls of your feet, and prepare to lunge or even jump forward as you make your stroke. This can be seen in Figure 26.

Notice how the receiver moves into the shot. The ball is actually hit with the legs and a short shoulder pivot. Jumping into the shot at the moment of impact, in this case, gives you a substantial source of controlled power.

You should hit the serve return flat or even with slice, but rarely, if ever, with heavy topspin. This is because the ball that you must hit is high and fast-moving, and topspin is difficult to apply when the ball is high. Moreover, topspin requires a longer swing, and the timing with top-

4

spin is more exacting than with a flat stroke.

A few more tips on the return of serve:

1. Get yourself energized and a little excited as you prepare to return. Open your eyes wide, bounce around, and try to conjure up positive feelings. Make yourself feel aggressive. Visualize moving your weight forward and driving the ball deep into your opponent's court. Convince yourself that you want your opponent to hit the serve in so you can attack it. Feeling defensive or hoping that your opponent will double fault will slow your reactions and lead to ruin.

2. Stay loose. In particular, keep your wrists flexible, so you can adjust to surprises. Trying too hard makes you stiff and slow so you must learn to reach a balance between relaxation and excitement. I call it a state of "relaxed excitement."

3. Focus on the ball. Watch it closely as your opponent throws it up, as he makes contact, and as the ball bounces off your court. There is a strong tendency to take your eye off the ball in the flurry of hitting the return and frequent mishits result. Take extra care to follow the ball from the time your opponent tosses it up until it has bounced on your side of the court.

4. Be aware that each player will be better at serving into some areas of the court than into other areas. Few players, for example, can slice serves wide and hit flat down the center with equal facility. As soon as possible, try to figure out which serves your opponent likes and where he is hurting you. Then move over to cover the serves he likes to hit. This will force him to choose between serving right into the spot where you are waiting or hitting serves he is not good at.

Mike White, a former player on my Pepperdine team, illustrates this point well. He had a devilish serve and drove his opponents to distraction with aces. But this only happened because people stood in the middle of the serve return area so that they could reach serves hit to either corner. Most of them never figured out that Mike's best serve, by far, was his slice into the forehand side, and this serve did most of the damage. Mike didn't want them to figure it out either, so he hit enough flat serves into his opponent's backhands to keep them guessing. But this was just a bluff. His money serve was into the forehand. Mike actually had difficulty serving into the backhand corners because he tossed the ball too far out to his right side and put a natural slice on the serve. Mike was in big trouble if a smart receiver moved over a step to his right so that he was ready for any serve Mike might hit to his forehand and simply dared Mike to serve to his backhand.

How do you know which serves your opponent likes best? An important clue is where he serves on the big points such as 30–40 or deuce. He will usually go with his best serve in these situations. Do not allow yourself to be victimized repeatedly by the same serve. Move over and be ready for your opponent's best serve on the next big point. (So you can, at least, be victimized by a different serve.)

You can sometimes anticipate the direction of your opponent's serve by observing his ball toss and stance. If he is a right-hander and throws the ball up to his right side, he will usually serve best to your forehand side. If his ball toss is more over his head, he will probably be better at serving to your backhand. I use words like *probably* and *usually* because if a server is good enough with his wrist, he can direct the ball anywhere with any ball toss.

If the server stands several feet away from the centerline, he can serve wide more easily. And the farther away from the centerline he stands, the wider he can serve. In this case you must move your stance out wider to cover wide serves. The farther he moves away from the centerline, the farther wide you must move. If you are forced to move several feet toward the sideline because of your opponent's stance, you may feel that you are leaving a lot of room for him to serve down the middle. Don't worry about it. This is a very difficult serve for him to hit when he is standing away from the centerline.

If your opponent remains on the baseline after serving, try to hit the return as deep as possible. Push him back in the court so you can take the offense. Many players are afraid to miss serve returns, so they get conservative and are hesitant to do more than just get the ball in play. But if you make a habit of hitting short, easy returns, your opponent will start out too many points by jerking you around, particularly at the higher levels of play. Of course, too many errors won't get you any trophies either, so you must ultimately strike a reasonable balance between aggression and consistency.

If your opponent serves wide, your highest percentage return is generally crosscourt, for the same reasons as with any ground stroke: The ball will pass over the low part of the net, there is more court into which you can hit, and you are in a better court position to reach your opponent's next shot. The down-the-line return is the aggressive but risky play.

This assumes, of course, that your opponent does not have a substantially weaker side. If he does, then it may pay to hit to his weak side, even though it may initially put you at a positional disadvantage.

If your opponent advances to the net behind his serve, you must keep your return low unless you plan to hit a winner. If your opponent serves wide, you can be aggressive and hit down-the-line, but your shot must be a winner or near-winner. This is because if your opponent reaches your shot with any level of comfort, he is in an excellent position to put away his first volley. On the other hand, with your opponent storming the net you are in no position to get overly conservative anyway. Since down-the-line is the shortest distance past the net rusher, the wide serve does provide a nice opportunity for the clean pass if you can get a handle on the serve return.

Hitting your return crosscourt over the low part of the net is the conservative play. Aim for the far sideline in the neighborhood of the service line. It is easier to keep the ball low crosscourt—since you are hitting over the low part of the net—and the volleyer has a poor angle from which to hit an immediate winner. You can also choose to hit the ball hard and go for the crosscourt passing shot.

Incidentally, the serve return is one of the few situations where the backhand slice can be used effectively as a passing shot. However, it must be hit sharply and with a flat trajectory. The slice can work here because the shot is executed off of a high-bouncing ball and is hit from relatively shallow in the court. The slice ordinarily does not work well as a passing shot because it cannot be hit hard off of a low ball and must travel too great a distance.

APPROACH SHOTS

There are two types of approach shots. One is produced by stopping, hitting a normal ground stroke, and following it forward, while the other is hit on the move. When you stop to hit your approach, you can hit it harder and more accurately, but you will not be able to get into volleying position as quickly. If you are a poor volleyer, stopping to hit your approach may be a good play. Hitting the ball hard and near the line will elicit the easy volley that you need. In a sense, you transfer most of the work done in putting the ball away to your approach shot, rather than your volley.

The moving approach, while it can't be hit as severely, gets you to the net quicker, where you can do the real damage with your volley. Like the serve return, hit the shot with an abbreviated backswing (see Figure 27). As always, shortening your backswing increases your control but costs you some decrease in power. It is a good trade-off because moving shots are harder to control than standing ones. You will not need as much power from your swing anyway, because you will get more of it from your legs as you move forward than on a standing ground stroke. Since the ball is contacted well inside the court, it will need to travel a shorter distance than normal. Hitting it too hard, particularly on low balls, puts it in danger of carrying over the baseline.

To hit a moving approach shot, it is crucial to prepare early by rotating your upper body as you move forward, well before you hit the stroke. As you run, therefore, your legs will be facing forward while your upper torso is turned sideways. This may feel awkward at first and will probably take some getting used to (see Figure 27).

FIGURE 27.
Moving approach shot.

1   2

 The shot should usually be hit down-the-line and as deep as possible. If you chose to hit it crosscourt, you must hurt your opponent more, since you will be temporarily out of position. You cannot afford, in this case, to allow your opponent to set up for the passing shot. He must be forced to misdirect or hit the ball up so that you can reach it with your volley and hit a winner.

 You should hit the moving approaches either flat or with slice. Topspin is not a good choice here because, in addition to making the ball bounce up and become an easier target, it requires a longer backswing, higher racket velocity, and is difficult to control. It is usually best to hit the ball flat on your forehand side and either flat or sliced off the backhand. If you hit the backhand with one hand, you will find it difficult to hit flat approaches on the move, so a slice is usually in order. Two-handers will find it helpful to develop a one-handed slice approach shot, because it is awkward to hit low backhands with two hands when you are on the move forward. In any case, try to hit with a flat trajectory and impart sufficient backspin to the ball so that it will

4   5

skid rather than bounce. A low, skidding ball makes the
passing shot very difficult.

Always try to relax when hitting an approach shot, particularly on the move. In this situation, you need the flexibility that only relaxed hands can provide. There is a
natural tendency to tighten up and press when hitting an
approach. Fear of your opponent's passing shot accentuates
this, and errors result. So make a conscious effort to relax
during the shot. Flow through the ball and stay loose.

A special situation occurs when your opponent hits the
ball very short, either with a drop shot or inadvertently.
You have to race forward and can barely reach it before it
bounces a second time. You must now hit a very low ball
from well inside the service line. How should you play this
shot? If your opponent in on the baseline, hit the ball
down-the-line as deep as possible. Because you will have to
hit the ball softly in order to get it up over the net and down
into the court, your opponent will certainly reach the ball,
so plan to finish the point with your volley. Don't worry.
Even though your shot may be quite soft, your opponent

will still have difficulty passing if your ball lands deep in the court and you are in good volleying position.

Play the shot differently, however, if your opponent happens to be at the net as you are charging forward. Now you should usually hit it crosscourt. Have no delusions. You are definitely in some trouble here, but you can, on occasion, shove the ball over the low part of the net and get it past an unwary opponent. The down-the-line shot is more difficult because the extra height of the net on the side makes more difference when you get this close to it.

An alternative is to lob down-the-line. This is particularly effective with your forehand over his backhand side and when your opponent starts to look for the little sharply angled crosscourt and moves forward to cut it off.

DROP SHOTS

Drop shots are diabolical in many ways. They give you a unique opportunity to win a point and insult your opponent at the same time. They can make tired or slow-footed opponents run. Just the threat of the drop shot can force your opponent to play closer than normal to the baseline and become vulnerable to the deep drive. Drop shots can disrupt an opponent's rhythm. Because they are, somehow, so demeaning and irritating, they can anger or otherwise break your opponents down psychologically.

I got a personal lesson in destruction by drop shot in the semifinals of the 1960 NCAA championship. My opponent was a bizarre character named Whitney Reed who was a specialist in the drop shot. His strokes were totally unorthodox. Whitney faced the net on ground strokes and took roundhouse swings at the ball. Instead of conventionally charging to the net and sticking volleys into the corners, he wandered into the no-man's-land between the service line and baseline and played cat and mouse with you. From there, he hit drop volleys or slithering angled volleys and, after pulling you to the net with him, lob volleys. Because his touch was so good and his strokes so weird, you could never tell when the drop shot was coming. You knew it would be soon, but not exactly when.

Needless to say, Whitney was very unpleasant to play against. (I was not the only player who found him so. In 1961 Whitney was ranked No. 1 in the United States and had wins over everyone in the world, including the likes of Rod Laver and Roy Emerson.) That day in the NCAA semis, we played in front of packed stands. Whitney, who could never resist the urge to entertain an appreciative audience, opted to provide the fans with an amusing puppet show. He ran me around more real estate than I ever realized could be contained within the boundaries of a tennis court.

Drop shots followed by lobs did most of the damage. The crowd loved it. Serious competitor that I was, I tried for everything. The crowd began to giggle. I guess people just look silly when their upper bodies and legs attempt to move in two different directions simultaneously. I had never been laughed at before in an important tennis match. Beads of nervous sweat began to appear on the back of my neck. Whitney had me completely befuddled and demoralized. I forgot about winning the match. All I wanted to do was get off the court to avoid further torment.

But a drop shot can be a two-edged sword. It is deceptive in every sense of the word. You must deceive your opponent as to when you plan to use the shot, but many players deceive themselves as well. It looks like the easiest shot in the world. It is not. When players get into trouble, the drop shot seems like a way to turn the tables in a hurry. It is not. Is is a very difficult stroke which should be used only in certain situations, and then only sparingly.

The drop shot is an easy shot to miss, and under pressure it is even easier to miss. The ball must clear the net by a narrow margin, land within a few feet of the net, and then die. This requires flexible and delicate work with the wrist and hand. It is a confidence shot and easiest to hit when you are ahead and feeling good. When you get nervous, angry, or feel pressured, your hands tend to stiffen and your touch evaporates.

You should attempt it only when the ball lands short in the court and you are in control of the point. The ball needs to be short in the court so it will only have to travel a short

1   2   3

FIGURE 28.
Forehand drop shot.

distance before reaching its destination. Since the drop shot must necessarily travel slowly through the air, you cannot hit it far without giving your opponent too much time to react and reach it. Moreover, it is very difficult to accurately control a ball hit so softly over any substantial distance. You should be in control of the point when you hit the shot because you will then be in position early and have the time to relax and deceive your opponent.

Some players attempt to drop shot when their opponents are running them around the court in an effort to turn the point to their advantage with one cunning masterstroke or end it quickly. It will end quickly, all right, but usually with an outright error or with their opponents ramming a setup down their throats.

An excellent ball to hit a drop shot on is one which moves slowly and lands near your service line. This is a situation where you have the option of driving the ball deep to either corner, hitting an approach shot, or hitting a drop shot. For deception, prepare as you normally would. Rotate your shoulders in preparation for a regular stroke, but take a short backswing, much as you would for an approach shot. Then relax your wrists and hands and swing down and through the ball at about a thirty-degree angle (see Figure 28).

Note the short follow-through. You should apply some slight amount of backspin to the ball to make it bounce more vertically than horizontally and die close to the net.

COVERING
THE COURT

11

Great champions have beaten their opponents with all kinds of strokes and strategies—with net attacks, steady baseline play, power, guile, offense, and defense. But the champions have one factor in common. They could all cover the court. They were able to move, by one means or another, quickly enough to reach virtually all of their opponent's shots. They all *appeared* to have excellent speed of foot.

But did they really run as fast as they looked? Surprisingly, the answer is no. If a race were held among the top 1,000 players in the world, the highest ranking ones could very well finish in the middle of the pack. But as a tennis player, that doesn't matter. The race would tell little about who was the fastest on court. Even if the race were a short sprint, its result would throw little light on the players' ability to cover court. Since most moves on court are a matter of only a few yards, it seems like raw acceleration should be the determining factor in getting to the ball. But of far greater importance are anticipation—knowing early where your opponent is likely to hit the ball—and the ability to change directions quickly while keeping your balance.*

Perhaps the best example I can mention is Pancho Segura. Segura was the second best player in the world for most of the 1950s (behind the incredible and virtually unbeatable Pancho Gonzales). Except for "Big" Pancho Gonzales, Segura made pâté out of everyone on the pro circuit during that time, including the likes of Ken Rosewall, Tony Trabert, Frank Sedgman, and Alex Olmedo—all great champions in their own right. Yet just looking at Segura, you would have figured he was doing well if he made it across the street without getting run down by a bus.

Pancho Segura did not look like your typical tennis player. A native of Ecuador, he had a large (and very handsome) head and torso, but short, spindly, bowed legs which had resulted from a childhood case of rickets. As he shuffled awkwardly onto the court, his body oscillating precariously from side to side, he appeared to have his hands full (or legs full) just walking, let alone running. At five-seven, facing the enormous serves and ferocious attacking games of his great opponents on lightning-fast indoor courts, it was clear that he had better be able to move.

Yet when play commenced, a magical transformation occurred. Pancho's scrawny, bent legs almost seemed to straighten out. The awkward look disappeared and Pancho got to every ball—easily. Wherever his opponent might

---

* Teaching pros sometimes become frustrated because their beginning pupils stand immobilized, like a deer with a light in its eyes, when the ball is coming. They scream, "Don't let the ball come to you, go get it!", "Move your feet!", or "Stop being so lazy!" But the pupil is not lazy at all; he simply does not know where to run. It takes time and experience for a tennis player to learn how to compute the ball's trajectory quickly and accurately. The beginner must observe the flight of the ball for a long time until he has accumulated enough data points to calculate where the ball will land. He dare not start running early because he has no idea yet *where* to run. On the other hand, an experienced professional can often compute the ball's complete trajectory by observing the initial foot or two of the ball's flight path, so it never occurs to him that his pupil might be having this type of difficulty.

hit, little Pancho was there, seemingly without effort or hurry. I doubt he could have beaten my grandmother in a fifty-yard dash, but on a tennis court there were few faster. How did he do it?

First, he knew *where* to run sooner than his opponent. He got the jump on the ball with his great mind. He understood the geometry of the court perfectly and knew, with unerring accuracy, the percentages of where his opponent might reasonably hit every ball. Because Pancho could tell where his opponent's stroke would be directed before the ball was actually struck, he was virtually always moving early and in the right direction. Therefore he was always on balance. Second, he started his move back to the center of the court extremely quickly after completing his own stroke. This gave him even more of a head start. And finally, he used his knowledge of court geometry and percentages to hit shots which did not unduly open up his court and expose him to long, difficult runs. Let me show you some of the secrets Segura used in covering the court.

Consider the geometry of the court. On the baseline this is a one-dimensional problem: lateral movement from sideline to sideline. If your opponent runs you wide, you must recover back toward the center of your court after completing your stroke. But it depends on where *you* hit the ball as to whether you will have an easy or difficult time getting to your opponent's next shot.

If, on the wide ball, you reply with a crosscourt, you need not recover all the way back to the center of the court. Only when your shot is hit to the center of your opponent's court need you return all the way to the center of your court. Note in Diagrams 23 through 25 that the wider your crosscourt return lands in your opponent's court, the farther away from the center your ideal recovery position (IRP) can be. Thus, the wider your return, the less distance you will have to run to reach your IRP.

Diagram 25

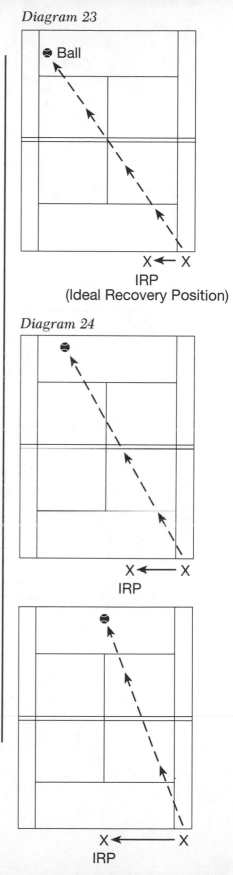

Diagram 23

IRP
(Ideal Recovery Position)

Diagram 24

IRP

IRP

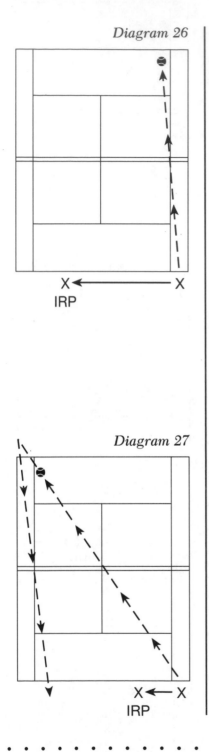

Diagram 26

X ←——————— X
IRP

Diagram 27

X ←— X
IRP

On the other hand, if you hit down-the-line, your IRP will be on the far side of the center line, requiring quite a long run (and a damn fast one, too; see Diagram 26).

If you have hit the ball deep or wide crosscourt and you recover to your IRP, in a sense you are daring your opponent to hit down-the-line because you leave room open along the down-the-line corridor (see Diagram 27).

Note that if your shot is hit wide enough, your opponent's best down-the-line reply will still be heading back into your court toward you. If your shot was hit deep crosscourt, your opponent will be forced to hit a great half-volley down-the-line in order to take advantage of your open court area and hurt you. And that is a difficult, low-percentage play.

The first prerequisite for superior court coverage is, therefore, to know the location of your IRP for every opponent and every court situation. And your IRP is not just a geometric function of where you hit the ball. It also depends on your opponent's strengths and weaknesses. For example, if you are facing an opponent with a great down-the-line shot, you will have to recover closer to the center of your court after hitting crosscourt from a wide position.

How does a player learn where his IRP is for all these situations? You start by becoming familiar with the basic percentages of shot selection and court geometry as described earlier. At the beginning this is an intellectual exercise. Then you must fine-tune this information and incorporate it into your unconscious mind by experience during practice and match play. If you are alert, you will learn quickly by reward and punishment. The process is to hit a shot, recover to your IRP (at least to your best estimate of where it is), and make a mental note of where your opponent usually hits his reply. Sometimes your opponent will hurt you with down-the-line shots and sometimes with crosscourt shots. Your IRP is that position along your baseline where these two shots hurt you about equally often. Ultimately, you will unconsciously feel where your IRP is.

Next you must try to get the jump on your opponent's shot by starting your recovery move early. Do this by making an extra effort to arrive in position for your shot *well before the ball arrives*. Ideally, you should reach a position slightly wide of your contact position and have your weight pulling back toward the center of your court as you make your hit. In that way your recovery begins even *before* you finish your stroke. Do not just arrive in position at the same time as the ball. If you do, your momentum will carry you laterally away from your IRP for a split second after your hit. And this will kill your recovery.

If you have to hit a wide forehand, use an open stance and push back to the center with your outside leg as you hit. If you have to hit wide backhand, you cannot use an open stance, but if you get outside of the ball and use a one-handed slice, you can still push back to the center off of your front foot during the hit. Then you step back toward the center with your back leg as shown in Figure 29. In this case you actually are moving backward for the first step.

It is more difficult to push back toward the center as you hit a flat or topspin backhand. These strokes require that you set up your position more firmly, hit the ball farther in front of you, and drive your weight forward at contact. This slows recovery and forces you to hit crosscourt more frequently or, if you do hit down-the-line, hit a very severe shot.

The next aid in speeding up your movement is to learn to anticipate your opponent's shots. As you recover back to the center of your court after your shot, keep your eyes glued to your opponent. You must practice watching him closely as you move in order to become sensitive to the small clues which give away the direction of his next shot. At first you will not notice the many tiny indications of his intentions. However, experience will teach you to unconsciously integrate these into a definite foreknowledge of where he is going to hit. They must be taken in as a whole—a gestalt. And the process begins immediately after you hit your shot.

As you move back into position after your shot, you will be constantly analyzing minuscule bits of information about your opponent's designs. And you must continue to recover position and accumulate information as long as possible before making any final decision as to where your opponent

FIGURE 29. *Recovery to the center after a wide backhand.*

THINK TO WIN

is going to hit the ball. Early in his preparation sequence for the stroke he can hit the ball anywhere. But as the sequence progresses, he gradually loses this ability. Just before making ball contact he becomes completely committed (although the great players can put off the instant of decision for an uncomfortably long time by using their wrists). Your certainty of where he will hit the ball will grow during the preparation sequence as your opponent's options diminish.

Finally, you will reach the instant of decision where you must pause for a split second as your growing feelings of shot direction develop into near-certainty. This is the instant in which one more step toward recovery will leave you vulnerable to being wrong-footed.

Basically, your opponent has two shot choices: (1) to hit into the open court, or (2) to wrong-foot you by hitting into the court area just vacated. Your problem, of course, is that you do not know which option he will choose. So just at the instant of decision you must hesitate in the ready position. This is facing the net, on the balls of your feet with your legs spread, and with your center of gravity lowered (knees bent). Now you can move in any direction—either continuing toward the open court or retracing your steps back to the area you just left. This ready-position pause lasts only a fraction of a second and hardly slows you down. You actually just bounce on the balls of your feet as you make a final determination of your opponent's shot direction and, almost in a continuous motion, drive yourself in the proper direction by pushing off hard with your outside leg (see Figure 30).

It is important that you not be running at the instant of decision. The split step and bounce out of the ready position can be done so quickly, once the timing has been mastered, that you will lose very little time when covering balls hit into the open court. And you will gain the ability to cover balls hit behind you with relative ease. These would be unreachable if you had continued to run in the wrong direction as your opponent hit.

The same technique—a split step and pause in the ready position—should be used at the net, when serving and

FIGURE 30. *Recovery and direction change.*

1

2

3

4

5

6

THINK TO WIN

volleying, or anywhere else you may be in the court at the instant of decision. If you happen to be far out of position, you must run like the devil to recover, but even if you are still well away from recovery at the instant of decision, you must still pause to ascertain where your opponent is going to hit the ball. In this desperate situation, when you are so far out of position that complete recovery is hopeless, there is a trick you can use which will sometimes salvage the point. You try to sucker your opponent into hitting to a spot of *your* choosing.

You might need to do this, for example, when your opponent has a high, easy volley and you are off near one of the sidelines—leaving your whole court open. Your problem is that you cannot possibly reach the far side of the court without instantly sprinting for it at full speed before your opponent hits the ball, running right through the instant of decision. This leaves your opponent leeway to watch you run and decide at leisure whether to hit into the opening or behind you into the wide area of recently vacated court.

Here's a trick which may save you. Start out moving toward recovery, but not at full speed. Then, just before your opponent must take his eyes off you in order to focus exclusively on the ball for his shot, accelerate forward with a flurry toward the open court. He will have already decided to hit into the open court because you left it open by moving toward recovery at less than full speed. But the last thing he now sees as he turns his full attention to the ball is you sprinting toward where he intends to hit. This may cause him to change his mind at the last instant (or, better yet, *after* the last instant) and try to wrong-foot you. This was exactly what you were trying to get him to do, of course, because your flurry toward the open court was just a feint. While your opponent takes his eyes off you and watches the ball, you turn and recover unseen toward the area you just left. If he falls for your ruse, he may miss the shot or hit an inaccurate one because he changed his mind so late. And you will be there to take advantage of it.

You can use a similar ruse at the net to influence your opponent's choice of shot. If you have hit short, leaving him lots of time to set up and too many easy options for passing shots, you can start drifting toward the center of the court instead of remaining positioned properly in front of the ball to cover the down-the-line pass. As your opponent is deciding where to hit his passing shot, he spies a fat, tempting hole open up down-the-line. At the instant he focuses on the ball before contact, you lunge to close up the hole. He must now thread the needle and hit a perfect down-the-line passing shot to get the ball by you. Anything less and you are there to angle the ball off with a crosscourt volley. Since he originally figured to have lots of room, he will have to make an instantaneous and difficult change of mentality— from a relaxed state with an easy shot to a focused state with a tough shot. If he can't make the change fast enough, you get him.

In contrast to baseline play, normal recovery at the net is a two-dimensional problem. (On the baseline, the problem is one-dimensional.) At the net you must recover forward and back as well as side to side. Why? Because your opponent has the option to lob as well as pass on either side of you. Proper lateral court position dictates that you be on the same side of the court as the ball, and proper lob coverage dictates that you be in the safe position, as first described in Chapter 6 on the volley. This safe position may be defined as the position *closest* to the net which still allows you to cover most of your opponent's lobs. Its exact location will depend on (1) how well your opponent lobs—if he is deceptive and accurate you must stand farther back; (2) how frequently your opponent lobs—if he seldom lobs you can crowd the net; (3) how much trouble you have put your opponent in with your approach shot or last volley—if you have hit deep and put him in trouble, you can stand closer to the net; (4) wind conditions—if it's blowing in your face, play closer; if it's blowing from behind you, play farther back.

Diagram 28 shows the two-dimensional nature of recovery at the net.

Note that if you have closed forward of the safe position and volleyed crosscourt, you must recover *both* by following the ball laterally *and* by backing up toward the safe position. Again, you must be sure to pause briefly in the ready position just at your opponent's moment of decision, even if you are still quite far out of position. Then you can lunge or run in any direction.

The exact location of the safe position is not always obvious at first. But the test is empirical—if your opponent is able to lob over your head more than *very* occasionally, you must remain a step farther back from the net. If the lobs continue to get over you, play farther back still. Eventually you will find a position where you are safe from any but the occasional great lob. I have seen players coming to the net with a strong wind at their backs bewildered by the fact that their opponents can lob over their heads repeatedly with ease, even though they are playing a step deeper than their normal safe position. They do not realize that under certain unusual conditions, the safe position may be at the service line. They are reluctant to play in such an abnormal position. But there would be no problem if they kept in mind that the test is always empirical—if your opponent is lobbing over your head, keep moving back until he no longer can. By the same token, if you are reaching all lobs comfortably, move a step forward and see if you can get away with it.

Diagram 28

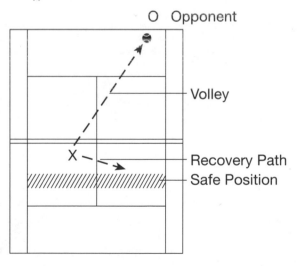

O Opponent

Volley

Recovery Path
Safe Position

GAME PLAN

12

Before playing the first point of a match, it is absolutely necessary to have in mind a game plan—a basic set of strategic guidelines for your play. It is, in fact, better to have a poor game plan than none at all. The game plan gives your efforts structure and direction, without which you are like a rudderless ship. Under pressure, it is your port in a storm. It provides the ledge to which you cling as the multitude of small disappointments in the match threaten to sweep you away. It gives you a baseline against which to measure the progress of the match. As new information comes in during the course of play, you adjust your plan to fit the changing situation.

Absent a game plan, a player just hits shots and lacks the wherewithal to mount a concerted attack or serious defense. The most telling sign of panic, discouragement, and breakdown in resolve is when a player discards his game plan and competes with tactics which change from point to point or without structured tactics at all. It is symptomatic of the beginning of the end.

A good example of what I mean occurred on my Pepperdine team. Pat, a freshman newcomer, was playing a challenge match against Roger, a veteran member of the team. Since the outcome of the match would determine their positions on the team, each had good reasons for wanting to win. They had been training extra hard for it all week, doing hours of drills, running, and physical conditioning.

In a sense, a team challenge match has even more pressure than a tournament. In the challenge there is a social and personal aspect to the result. Here you play a teammate who you must see all the time. And since your social status on a team is somewhat determined by your position, it is a lot more pleasant playing ahead of someone rather than behind him. With a tournament, on the other hand, you can take a loss and simply forget it. Pat desperately wanted to establish himself by winning the match and Roger, just as desperately, wanted to hold his position and stay ahead of the new kid.

Although he was young, Pat had a developed and well-balanced game, with a solid serve, sound ground strokes, and an excellent volley. As the match began, Pat used a medley of tactics. He served and volleyed; he worked Roger around the baseline; he advanced to the net from short balls; he even mixed in some surprise approaches to the net on Roger's second serve.

Roger, meanwhile, had a simpler plan. He hit the ball as consistently deep as he could and waited for Pat to hit a short ball. Every time one landed near the service line, Roger hit an approach shot and went to the net. His intention was to break down Pat's ground strokes with a persistent net attack.

For most of the first set, the contestants battled on even terms. Then, as the pressure mounted, Pat momentarily faltered and Roger managed to eke out a close first set. As the second began, Pat started to look confused. He wasn't sure exactly why he lost the first set or what to do about it. He started to hit a little harder to put more pressure on Roger and keep him away from the net, but made more errors. He tried coming to the net more himself, but picked the wrong times, looked off balance, and missed volleys.

Meanwhile, Roger's confidence grew as Pat's withered.

His passing shots improved, making Pat's forays to the net even more precarious. Soon Pat did not dare come to the net at all, and, pinned on the baseline, he was a sitting duck for Roger's net attacks. Frustration grew and mistakes multiplied. The second set did not last long, and Pat walked off a disheartened loser. "All that practice and hard work down the drain," he muttered. "I tried as hard as I could, but my shots were just not good enough." Pat, however, could not have been further from the truth.

The problem had nothing to do with Pat's shotmaking abilities or consistency. It was that he had no solid game plan. And without one, he fell apart as soon as he ran into trouble. Pat had no clear conception of how he intended to go about winning points. He was trying, all right, but trying to do what? It is useless to simply chase around after balls and diffusely "try." One must specifically try to do *something*. Was he trying to outsteady Roger and win points because Roger missed before he did? Or was he attempting to attack and win by putting balls away from the net? He lost because he could not have answered these questions.

To understand the importance of a game plan, it may help to look at a classic example from the history of warfare. That's not as absurd as it may seem. In a fundamental sense, the tactics of warfare and tennis are similar. Both ultimately rely on breaking down the opponent's will and organization. Once this happens, the opponent becomes easy prey.

In tennis the organization is mental and embodied in a game plan; in warfare it is physical and appears in the formations of the armies. Battles in ancient Greece, for example, were fought by opposing forces lined up in a rectangular array of lines and columns, called a phalanx. The men in each line were protected by shields and armed with spears and short swords. They fought shoulder to shoulder and relied for strength and protection on maintaining their formation. When a man in the front fell, he was immediately replaced by the man behind him so the line could remain intact.

As long as it held together, this tactic presented an extremely formidable fighting machine. All the enemy could see was a forest of shields and spears. As long as the two phalanxes clashed head-on and did not waver, casualties were taken about equally. Havoc ensued only if one line broke. When one army turned and ran or started to mill around without structure, the intact army could use its weapons on the unprotected backs and sides of its enemies. Now it was able to inflict fantastic numbers of casualties while suffering virtually none itself. Battle strategies always had the same basic goals—to break up the enemy's formation, cause panic, and then destroy him when he became too disorganized to protect himself.

Success in a tennis match also relies on breaking down the structural integrity of your opponent's game while, of course, maintaining your own. A player's game plan functions like an army's formation in giving the player a relatively impervious platform from which to launch attacks or mount defenses. It serves as a template for resolve. During match play a competitor must focus all his energies on executing his game plan properly. At the same time, he must do everything he can to convince his opponent that *his* game plan is a losing one.

In tennis, as in battle, this can be done in two basic ways—by brute force (as in a frontal assault), or by guile (as in a flank attack or envelopment, where the strike is against the enemy's vulnerable sides or rear).* When a competitor attacks with brute force, he pays little attention to his opponent's weaknesses. He simply uses his own strengths over and over like a bludgeon and assumes that his opponent cannot resist indefinitely. The more devious methods of guile make an opponent's weaknesses the focus of the onslaught. Both methods are based on the hope that if the

* It was with an envelopment that the great Hannibal, with his mixed force of 50,000 Carthaginians and auxiliaries, was able to nearly annihilate a veteran Roman army of 80,000 legionnaires at Cannae in the most famous battle of antiquity. Fifty thousand Romans were left dead on the field at a cost to Hannibal of less than 5,000 men. It seems incredible that so many men could be killed in hand-to-hand combat with so few casualties to the other side. But poor planning and, ultimately, panic led to disaster for the Romans.

tactics work well enough, an opponent will lose commitment to his own failing plan and be unable to replace it with a better one. As in battle, demoralization, disorientation, and disintegration is the result.

A game plan is a funny animal. It must be taken seriously enough to commit your full mental energy to its execution, yet not so seriously that it is rigid and you cannot adjust it. When the match begins, you should adopt the first draft of a plan based on everything you know up to that point. If you know nothing about your opponent, construct a plan based on your own strengths and weaknesses. Then commit to it with all the intensity you can muster.

At the same time—and this is the tricky part—*without* diminishing your commitment to your plan you have to monitor the progress of the match and assess whether it is working. Does it feel good to you? Are you in control? Are you winning? If it feels good, stick with it. It is only if you are losing and feel out of control or dominated that you must seriously consider making a game plan change.

The great champion Bill Tilden is credited with coining the old adage, "Always change a losing game; never change a winning one." This makes great sense, but the hook comes when you try to determine what constitutes a losing game. If you lose two points in a row, does that mean you are playing a losing game? What if you lose two games or a set? I suppose if you wait until you actually lose the match you could be *sure* it was a losing game, but that, somehow, does not ring smart. So the first question to ask yourself is, "Could this be just a temporary condition?"

Think about the last time you started out a match hitting the ball in an effortless manner and with exceptional accuracy. You may even have jumped to a four- or five-game lead. But in your heart of hearts you knew that you were playing above your abilities—your game was levitating—and the party could end at any instant.

You probably will not have to search far into your memory banks to recall the many times your touch evaporated at this point and allowed your opponent to come back and beat you. It is like the cartoon character who is moving so fast that he runs past the edge of the cliff and manages to keep going for a while on thin air. Then he stops, realizes he is doing the impossible, and falls into the canyon below.

In a similar manner, matches are not always what they appear to be initially. Sometimes an opponent is having a hot streak, but cannot really sustain it. Or, even if your opponent is playing within his capabilities, time is a factor in any strategic equation. There is a finite time limit to any player's ability to maintain concentration and resolve. An opponent may be better than you for thirty minutes or an hour. But that doesn't mean he will be better than you after two or three hours. The effort to maintain full concentration is draining, as are the multitude of vicissitudes and small disappointments inherent in hard-fought match play. Everyone tires mentally if he is forced to concentrate long enough.

The great players can sustain their mental energy for four or five hours, but even they will crack eventually. The recreational players, on the other hand, will crack a lot sooner. I have seen an undergunned Brad Gilbert drag down the great Boris Becker on several occasions by simply making each point and game as painful as possible and keeping Becker on the court for a long time. Becker may have started out playing well, but by the end of the match he looked as frustrated as Brer Rabbit fighting the tar baby. It is not always necessary to change game plans or even to have the stronger game to bring your opponent to this point.

Most players make the mistake of giving up on a game plan too quickly or changing it too drastically. There are no hard and fast rules here. But in general, as soon as things start to go wrong, most players suspect their strategy is at fault; they get panicky and emotional. In this state of mind their play naturally deteriorates, even if their game plan is essentially correct. Feeling impelled to change tactics, they often jump from the frying pan into the fire by adopting a new plan which is worse than the first. Before long they have tried and discarded a number of plans and finally run out of ideas.

Even top professionals occasionally fall prey to this type of error. In the Nabisco Masters Championship in 1988

Andre Agassi started out giving Ivan Lendl a good flogging on the baseline. Dominating completely with his ground strokes, Agassi won the first set 6–1. In the process Agassi jerked Lendl around the court so violently that if Lendl had been paying a fitness trainer he would have felt he got a bargain. As the second set unfolded, Agassi still controlled the baseline, but Lendl held even by virtue of some inspired serving at crucial points. The set went to a tiebreaker, which Lendl won by a whisker to even the match at a set apiece.

At this stage Agassi inexplicably decided on a change of game plan. He started to serve and volley as well as mix in some net attacks behind his ground strokes. Since Agassi neglected to take into account the fact that he doesn't know how to volley, he was, predictably, cut to shreds in the final set. He had made two cardinal errors in tactics: He changed a reasonable game plan too soon, and, more disastrously, adopted a plan which was almost impossible for him to execute successfully.

Let us assume it is clear to you that your initial game plan is a losing one. What kind of change should you make? The most important detail to keep in mind—and it seems almost too obvious to mention—is to be sure the new plan is *within your capabilities*. Simple as this may seem in the unemotional surroundings of your living room, on the court it is often overlooked, with, as Andre Agassi found out, disastrous consequences.

I recently witnessed a common example of how this can happen in a tournament match between Bill and Fred at my local tennis club. They are both baseline players and started out trading ground strokes in long rallies. The first set was close, but Bill took it and appeared to be gaining the upper hand in the second. Fred became convinced that Bill was too steady for him and decided, therefore, on a change of game plan. He realized that he could not mount an effective net attack because his volley was too weak, so he elected to become very aggressive off the ground. He started hitting the ball hard and close to the lines. He also started missing more and quickly went down in flames in the second set.

In Fred's mind he felt justified in taking greater risks because he needed to get rid of a game plan that was leading to defeat. Unfortunately for him, he picked an alternative plan which was beyond his capabilities. Fred (or anyone else, for that matter) can hit the ball only so hard and still maintain enough control to limit his errors to an acceptable level. If he hits outside of this "power range," he will miss so many shots that only a miracle could save him.

Of course, it is always possible that Fred could get hot enough to pull it off—it is also theoretically possible that all the oxygen molecules in the room could move away from you at once, end up in the corner, and you would be asphyxiated—but I wouldn't bet on either one of these things happening. Fred's confusion was in what the concept of *capabilities* means. He thought a plan was within his capabilities if he could pull it off at least once every ten years or so. I define it as attempting only those plans which will not lead to a substantial increase in your error rate. And hitting outside of your power range will do just that, so it can never be included in a viable alternative game plan.

What, then, could Fred have done to increase his chances of winning? Fred's obligation as a competitor was to try to find the game plan which gave him the best chance of winning, even if this chance was less than even. (I would, for example, prefer a one-in-five chance of winning to a one-in-ten chance.) Maybe the best Fred could have done that day was to keep trying to outsteady Bill. He was likely to lose, but when he adopted his "slug for the lines" strategy he became a lot more likely to lose. It should have been clear to Fred, as he was being slaughtered after making the change, that his new plan was worse than his original. So why didn't he simply return to the original? Because he did not adopt the new plan to maximize his probability of victory. He did it, rather, out of discouragement with the way the match was progressing. He felt he was going to be beaten anyway, so he had nothing to lose.

That was a mistake, a mistake a lot of tennis players make. They do not realize that tennis is a game of probabilities, not certainties. Nothing is for sure in tennis, only for "maybe." Your strategic objective in match play is to maximize your probability of victory. But until the match is over, you will never be certain of winning, just as you will never be certain of losing. (For some perverse reason, however, most people feel a lot more certain of losing when they are behind than they feel certain of winning when they are ahead.) In any case, by turning to a game plan which he could not execute, Fred was really throwing in the towel. In general, when players adopt strategies that are outside their capabilities, it is often simply their covert way of quitting.

As an alternative, Fred might have tried hitting some soft, high ground strokes to break up Bill's rhythm, or some drop shots. But in any case Fred should have made only those changes that could *increase his chances of winning the match,* not no-chance, desperation changes because he was on his way down the tubes. And the way to be sure you're doing that is to accurately monitor the results of any change.

The great players are *immediately* sensitive to what works. They are drawn to a successful tactic like a shark to blood and recoil from a losing one as if it were the touch of a hot poker. The losers seem to embrace the effective and ineffective with mindless democracy. Fred should have seen that the change was not working and tried another or reverted to trying to outsteady Bill. Maybe the second time around he would have done better.

It is rare that an original single game plan remains completely intact for an entire match. Often it must be adjusted several times during a mtach to take advantage of opportunities that arise or to counter adjustments made by your opponent which are hurting you. Let us look in on Brad Gilbert's match with Mats Wilander in the first round of the 1990 U.S. Open to see this in action.

Brad started out with the intention of trading ground strokes and maneuvering with Mats until he got a short ball and then attacking at the net. He planned to win points with a combination of consistency and volley winners. And for a few games they sparred on an even basis until Brad spied a weakness—Mats's forehand was missing or falling short in the court. Brad immediately began diverting more balls to the forehand side. He served and volleyed on Mats's forehand and worked to get into forehand crosscourt exchanges. When Mats was pulled wide and returned the ball short, Brad smacked the ball into the open court and came to the net. Mats was not able to control the passing shot well while on the dead run, and Brad won a number of points on misdirected attempts. Brad was on to a good thing and pulled ahead in the match, but Mats was not about to take it lying down.

He countered by stepping up the power on his own serve and following it to the net. He also became more aggressive with his ground strokes in order to take control of the points and get to the net before Brad. Now, forced to defend himself, Brad no longer had the leisure to pick Mats's forehand apart. The match balance swung toward Wilander. But Brad soon adjusted to the new reality. By notching up the power on his serve returns and ground strokes, he was able to blunt much of Mats's new attack and retain a degree of offense himself. This was enough to even the momentum of the match, and Brad's initial lead was enough to allow him to squeak through in four close sets.

One can clearly see reason and experience at work in these various tactical adjustments. Neither player became overly emotional during the contest, so each change was coldly calculated. Both were well aware of any relative advantage or disadvantage and responded with small, carefully controlled adjustments. They were obviously in tune with the effectiveness of whatever they or their opponent did. At the end both had developed optimum game plans for this particular situation, and the outcome was ultimately determined by who could execute better.

I put into practice the advantages of game planning with my Pepperdine University team. Before they ever go on court against a rival school, we have a meeting in which each match is discussed and a game plan is developed. I'd like to take you through the thought processes for one match as an example of how this works. Let's use the aforementioned Pat, and Jason, a member of rival UCLA's squad.

Pat's game, as you may remember, is well balanced. Jason, on the other hand, is a super-consistent baseline specialist. Jason's forehand is his stronger side and his second serve is a definite weakness. For openers we had to decide how Pat was going to win his points, and there were, as always, only two possibilities: either Jason misses or Pat hits a winner. Since Jason makes his living hitting consistent ground strokes, a pivotal fact to keep in mind was that Jason had the advantage on the baseline. If it were to come down to a simple matter of consistency, Pat would be likely to miss first. Pat, therefore, had to win with offense, attacking Jason at the net. The only question remaining was how to go about it in the face of Jason's strong passing shots.

The focus of Pat's attack was going to have to be Jason's backhand, since that was his weaker side. Pat planned to hit the majority of his serves as well as his approach shots there. In addition, if Pat was at the net and found himself unable to hit a winning volley, he would, if possible, volley into Jason's backhand side. This type of consistent pressure on Jason's backhand might, as a bonus, even cause it to break down and spew forth a stream of errors.

A second part of Pat's plan was to go after the glaring weakness in Jason's second serve. He'd stand in close, hit aggressive returns, and, on occasion, use his serve return to come to the net. This would get Pat to the net immediately so he would not become embroiled in long baseline rallies he was likely to lose. In addition, it might make Jason uncomfortable enough to induce some double faults. If Jason's serve broke down, it might act like a hole in the dike, causing deterioration in other parts of his game. Pat also planned to come to the net behind his own first serve and on any ground stroke which Jason hit that landed near the service line.

During the course of the match Pat was going to have to adjust his attack according to the effectiveness of Jason's passing shots. If they were better than expected, Pat would have to come to the net behind stronger approach shots. But Pat had to realize that no matter what changes he made, he could under *no* circumstances give up his net attack entirely and stay on the baseline with Jason. His ground strokes were simply not good enough.

In reviewing the development of Pat's game plan, the following general principles are apparent: (1) One must first gain a clear understanding of one's own and one's opponent's relative strengths and weaknesses; (2) then decide on a *general* plan of how you intend to win most of your points. The question you must answer here is whether you are better off with offense or defense. You must choose between forcing the play in order to hit winners yourself, or playing consistently and waiting for your opponent to make errors. (In Pat's case, his general plan was to take the offense with a net attack.) (3) Finally, decide specifically how to carry out this general plan. (Pat's specific plan was to come to the net on Jason's backhand, second serve, and short ground strokes.)

Your specific plan will normally involve applying constant pressure to an opponent's weakness, either by attacking it or by outsteadying it. You hope, thereby, to break the weak stroke down. And if this happens, his strong strokes will probably falter as well. Every part of your game does not have to be better than your opponent's for you to break him down. All you have to do is find an exchange where you have a relative advantage and work on it over and over until your opponent cracks.

Again, there is an analogy with warfare. Alexander the Great's favorite tactic was a ferocious frontal assault. He used this with tremendous success, even against armies that outnumbered his by more than ten to one. His plan was to apply overwhelming force to a particular point in his enemy's line, destroy that section of the line, and create a panic which would spread throughout the enemy army. Once this happened, the opposition would scatter and run, and superior numbers would no longer do them any good. Alexander could wipe them out at leisure. And so too in tennis, you can sweep to victory if you can overwhelm an opponent's weakness and cause him to panic or lose heart.

If the game plan does not seem to be working, modifications should be considered *first* in the specific tactics used to carry out the general plan. In Pat's case this would mean figuring out other ways to get to the net or trying some attacks on Jason's forehand. The general plan should be maintained unless the player decides that its underlying assumptions are false or that discarding it will yield a higher probability of success. In Pat's case, again, the underlying assumption was that Jason was too steady for him on the baseline. He was left, therefore, with no alternative but to attack. The only reasons he would ever opt to battle Jason from the baseline would be: (1) He learns that Jason is *not*, in fact, steadier than he is, or (2) he finds he is being beaten so badly on offense that even though he is disadvantaged on the baseline, he is *less* disadvantaged than at the net.

The main points to bear in mind when you are contemplating making changes in your game plan are:

1. Stay cool and unemotional so that you can bring clear-headed intelligence to bear on the problem.
2. Change your game plan because you optimistically hope your new plan will be *better* than your old one, not because you simply wish to dive over the side of a sinking ship.
3. Pursue your new plan with all the will, energy, and enthusiasm you can muster.

In the final analysis, victory is a matter of execution. Although a good game plan can be a big help, any well-executed plan has a reasonable chance of succeeding. But no poorly executed plan will work, no matter how smart it is.

TACTICS

13

The strategies we've discussed up to this point fall under the categories of basic or general strategies. This chapter deals with more specific plans for putting your strokes and talents to work exploiting your opponent's soft underbelly, or, just as importantly, protecting your own. Some of these will be helpful in setting up game plans for matches. Others are tactical tips to be used in specific situations where they make sense. Since all competitive situations are in many respects different, all these ideas will not be appropriate in every match. In fact, some may even appear contradictory. I am simply describing here a collection of tactics that I have, at one time or another, found effective in my own matches.

As a general rule, matches hinge on your ability to use your strengths to exploit your opponent's weaknesses. At the same time, you try to hide your own weaknesses and stay away from his strengths. He, of course, is trying to do the same thing to you. It is analogous to a contest between two gladiators. Each maneuvers so that his opponent sees nothing but shield, while, at the same time, he works to bring his sword into play.

The wisdom of this should be obvious, but at one time I had a superbly talented player on my Pepperdine team who frustrated me beyond endurance by taking exactly the opposite approach. Roger (not his real name) perversely insisted on hiding his strengths and using his weaknesses. (As a professional, by the way, he has found it to be an excellent means of avoiding income tax problems.) Roger was blessed with an excellent serve and abilities at the net sufficient to gladden the most jaded coach's heart. Unfortunately, Providence's bounty did not extend to his ground strokes. He could hit them awfully hard, but there was too frequently some doubt as to where they might land. Yet if Roger got passed a few too many times for comfort, he would stop coming to the net and trade ground strokes for a while. He said his plan was to "break up my opponent's rhythm" or "to work my way in." Roger did not take into account the fact that his opponents were more likely to work their ways in on him or break up *his* rhythm rather than the other way around.

Watching Roger's wonderful game being repeatedly turned into confetti was one of the most frustrating experiences of my coaching career. Nothing I said made any difference. Roger was at that stage of a young person's life in which decisions are dictated by hormones rather than the central nervous system. He *wanted* to hit ground strokes. I don't enjoy it, but I can accept it if my players are beaten by someone who simply plays better. It's quite another matter to stand by as your player adopts a strategy that's suicide on the court.

Frequent losses to players with far less ability were Roger's punishment for ignoring rule number one: *Use your strengths and hide your weaknesses.* He permitted players with good ground strokes to get to his weak ones. His problem was not having weak ground strokes; it was allowing his opponents access to them. In fact, there have been world champions with ground strokes worse than Roger's, but they were less sporting in that they never hit them unless they absolutely had to. Alex Olmedo (Wimbledon champion, 1959) and Rafael Osuna (U.S. champion, 1963) hardly had ground strokes worthy of the name. They countered this deficiency by simply not letting the ball bounce very often. They came in on their own serves as well as their opponents', and if they faced a serve too big to come in on immediately, they slipped in at the first possible opportunity. People had trouble *finding* their ground strokes; every time they looked up, they saw Alex or Rafael at the net. And oh, how they could volley and cover the net.

Poor Roger, on the other hand, could never quite grasp the concept that if you are not good at a shot, you should do everything in your power to avoid hitting it in a match. The same concept holds true in other sports. For example, some years ago I was watching Magic Johnson put on a basketball clinic for a group of kids. He was demonstrating his skills playing a one-on-one game against another pro player who was several inches shorter than he was. Over and over Magic worked the ball in close to the basket and slipped in short shots. After a while, the kids wanted more action and started yelling, "Take some long ones, Magic. Pop from the outside." Magic stopped the game and held up his hand for silence. "Listen, you guys," he said. "I'm not a great outside shot. But I'm bigger than this guy, and I'm better than him around the basket. If I take him inside, I'll beat him all afternoon. But if I get stupid and try a bunch of shots from the outside that I'm not good at, I'll just lose. And I like winning. Remember, nobody is good at everything. You win by doing things you're good at and lose by doing things you're not."

In tennis, if you have to use your weakness, don't try to do too much with the shot. Consider the use of a weak shot as an interlude to be endured until, as soon as possible, you can bring your strengths to bear. For example, if you have a strong forehand and weaker backhand, plan to be consistent with your backhand while depending on your forehand to do your damage.

And even though your ground strokes are normally of the strength, there will be times when you simply lose confidence in either your forehand or backhand. It may happen during the course of a match or you may just start out the match that way. It is an uncomfortable feeling. Every time you hit a shot with the affected stroke, you have an abnormal doubt as to whether the ball will go in the court. You find that if you hit the ball at your normal pace, you make too many errors, and your quandary becomes, should you keep hitting at your normal pace and assume that your form will return, or should you ease up on the power in order to keep the ball in the court?

In my experience, it is best to ease up and hit the ball in the court. I have found that if you are fearful of a stroke and you try to press it anyway, you become extremely likely to miss. And this starts a bad cycle. The missing causes you to lose more confidence in the stroke, and this, in turn, causes you to make even more errors.

If you hit the ball easier, clear the net by a greater margin, stay away from the lines, and play high-percentage shots rather than tricky ones, you will make fewer errors. Try to work on the fundamentals of the stroke—watching the ball, preparing early, and relaxing during your swing. Coupled with hitting a lot of balls in the court, this will build your confidence in the stroke and eventually allow you to start increasing your power. In the meantime, rely on your other strokes to put pressure on your opponent and keep you in the match.

Though every player is different, the same general theory holds for all players: *Be aware of what you do better and worse than your opponent*, and base your strategy accordingly. To do that, you have to be sensitive to who has the best of it in various matchups. For example, if your forehand is your weaker side, it may still pay you to trade forehands crosscourt with your opponent if his is even worse than yours. Similarly, a poor volleyer may still get some mileage out of coming to the net if his opponent's passing shots are his weak point. This play especially should be considered when a ground stroker is being beaten by a persistent volleyer. Going to the net first in this case will not only deny the net to the volleyer, but the baseliner's net play may also have an advantage over the ground strokes of his opponent.

All players have points of weakness, and your game plans should revolve around how and when you exploit them.

Almost everyone, for example, has a weaker side. Even if an opponent's forehand and backhand appear at first to be equivalent, it will almost invariably turn out that they are not. Your most vital task is to determine, as early as you can (preferably in the prematch warm-up) which is your opponent's softer side. Some of the telltale signs of weakness are a late backswing, a stroke that looks awkward, a stroke that is often mishit, one that occasionally misses by a wide margin, and one that is hit primarily with the arm rather than the body.

Once identified, the weakness becomes your point of attack. It is the chink in his armor that can erode the remaining strong parts of his game. Exactly how you exploit this weakness depends on how bad it is. If it happens to be very poor relative to your opponent's good side, play it to death. It won't get better with exercise.

In my own case, the forehand was shaky. I hit it with an open stance, hard, and with heavy topspin. It looked dangerous. But I lacked confidence in the shot and, if it was tested persistently, it was prone to error. Those were the days of light balls, fast courts, and serve-volley attacks. My main tactic was to whack the forehand and pray that enough went in to bluff my opponent over to my backhand side, where I could really hurt him. I hated playing guys who figured out my forehand deficiency and couldn't be shaken off that side. Strangely enough, it didn't happen very often.

One time it did I was playing in a tournament against Dave Reed, a hot new freshman from my alma mater, UCLA. My old college coach, J. D. Morgan, knew about this weakness, of course, since we spent four years agonizing over it together. It was soon clear that Dave had been well briefed on my failings by my old mentor. His big serve found its way to my forehand like a plant seeks sunlight. (Instead of geotropism, I faced forehandtropism.) Worst of all, I knew that Dave *knew*! I was not going to be able to con him away from my forehand with my usual ruses. My throat constricted with the growing realization that I was going to be forced to hit forehand passing shots all match. Contrary to popular opinion, under these circumstances, practice does *not* make perfect. In fact, it served to destroy every vestige of confidence I had in my forehand. Before long, my forehand sunk to depths normally plumbed only by research submarines.

Under such an attack, the rest of my game might have broken down as well had I been younger and less experienced. However, time had taught me to confine my worries to the affected stroke and concentrate as usual on the other parts of my game. I was still able to serve and volley, so I focused on holding serve in an effort to keep the match even. Ultimately, at 7–8 in the first set, with Dave serving, we got into a long game. Maybe his youth was responsible, but at this crucial juncture, Dave opted to modify his single-minded attack on my forehand by mixing in a few timely (for me—untimely for him) serves into my backhand. That was all the opening I needed. I hit a couple of sharp returns and took the set. In the second set, Dave relaxed his deathlock on my forehand and I won the set more comfortably.

The tactical lessons to be learned from this anecdote are:

1. A severe weakness will usually get worse as a match progresses if it is played relentlessly.
2. It is often helpful if your opponent knows you are aware of his weakness and intend to exploit it. This makes him worry, lose confidence, and miss.
3. The more important the point, the more you should play to the weakness. It is most likely to break down in the pressure situation. The strength is likely to hold. In my match with Dave, he picked the worst possible time to start fooling with my backhand—just when the pressure was greatest and my forehand was the most liable to crack.

Even when the weaker side is not, as it was in my case, substantially worse than the other side, it should still be attacked on the bigger points. In addition, you should work it intelligently throughout the match, mining it like your private gold mine to produce consistent dividends. By doing so, you force your opponent to play a guessing game with you: "*when* am I going to hit to the weakness which we both know you have?" In this way you render your opponent a little tentative and off balance all the time. Better still, he is anticipating and reacting to what you do or may do, rather than thinking nasty thoughts about exploiting *your* weaknesses.

Sometimes you can even *create* a weakness when an opponent hits substantially the same from both sides. In my experience, particularly at the higher levels of the game, it's best to pick on the forehand because it is usually more dependent on confidence than the backhand. The latter is generally a more mechanically sound stroke, though less aggressive, and is the customary focus of attack. Zeroing in on the forehand tends to be a more surprising and thought-provoking tactic, and this can break down your opponent's confidence in the stroke. (At the recreational level the backhand is usually an obvious weakness, so you don't have to bother creating one. You already have one for free.)

To break down an opponent's forehand, simply start hitting a lot of extra balls to it. Serve to the forehand for a while, even if some of the returns are at first quite good. Hit balls to the forehand that your opponent would normally expect on his backhand. Let it be obvious. Your objective is to make him think, because in tennis matches, as in any sport, thinking and worrying are perilously close to interchangeable. Once your opponent starts having thoughts like "Hey, this fellow seems to be going after my forehand. Does he think it's weak or something?" you are likely to become the happy beneficiary of a complete breakdown.

Persistently attacking a weakness or attacking what your opponent otherwise considered a strength helps you to dominate your opponent, and this is always a good thing to do. Whenever possible, you want to call the tune in a match, rather than dance to your opponent's melody. When you can psychologically dominate your opponent, he will feel weak and is apt to lose resolve at some stage of the match. This, of course, will be his undoing.

To speed up this process, never let your opponent know he has hurt you in any way. If you can project an image of overwhelming force from across the net, it will help make your opponent feel ineffectual. And that may induce him to press his game in a vain effort to hear you yelp. In my day, Stan Smith was the master of this technique. He had one of the best tennis minds in the world. Although Stan was big, fast, and strong, he was not a great hitter of the ball. He stormed the net whenever he could and pounded his ground strokes the rest of the time, but lacked the slick shots of Arthur Ashe or Rod Laver. Yet he dominated the world for some years because he was such a great compet-itor. Stan exuded self-confidence. Nothing his opponent did made the slightest impression on him. He never changed his walk, his serene expression, or his attacking game plan. I played him many times and nobody else in the world ever made me feel so helpless. No matter what I did, Stan always appeared to have the answers. Against him I became frustrated, desperate, and ultimately missed easy shots because I felt I had to press my game.

You too can appear more resistant to your opponent's efforts on the court. In particular, if you get outsteadied in a long rally or two, do not immediately concede the base-line to your opponent by forcing play with harder strokes or desperate net attacks. This alerts him that you think he is too steady for you and will cause his stamina to increase in subsequent baseline rallies. Even if you ultimately decide he is too steady, keep playing long points until you win one—*then* change to a better strategy. In this way you overtly concede nothing.

The same principle holds in other circumstances, such as where you hit your serve. What if you serve to your oppo-nent's forehand and he cracks a blistering winner? "Oh-oh," you might think, "I'd better go to his backhand." Not so fast. In so doing you would send the message, "My, you have an awfully strong forehand. Because it frightens me so much, I'd better start serving to your backhand." This makes you look weak and will certainly not make anyone feel dominated. Therefore, you should, if possible, serve the next ball right into his forehand again. (If the next point is crucial and you coolly judge the percentages to be against the serve to the forehand, serve his backhand, but at the first opportunity go after his forehand again.) Now you are telling him, "That last forehand was awfully lucky. Can you hit another? I personally doubt it." Since he probably can't, this will not make him feel good. Again, if you decide after a while that serving to the forehand should generally be avoided, abandon serving that side at *your* pleasure, not in direct response to a good shot by him. And don't forget to serve an occasional ball to his forehand (on the less important points, of course), just to keep him guessing.

Since tennis is a game of errors, it is important to recognize that even if you are an attacking player, you will win most of your points because your opponent misses. Whenever possible, therefore, you want to *force your opponent to try difficult rather than easy shots* by reducing the amount of court into which he can comfortably hit. How can you accomplish this miracle? Simple. Call all balls out that land within a foot of the line. (No—I'm just kidding.)

One way to force your opponent to hit more difficult shots is to come to the net on short balls, even if you are a defensive player and even if you lose a few more points than you win. These aggressive moves raise your opponent's tension level. When you go to the net, your opponent on the baseline is under pressure to make a good shot lest you put the ball away. Whether he wins the point or not, a player will instinctively try to avoid the feeling of being pressured. He will therefore try to hit the ball deeper to keep you from coming in on him, and this means he is not free to just hit the ball anywhere in the court he pleases. Trying to hit into a smaller area of court will increase his errors.

Another cardinal rule is that *when you have your opponent in trouble, don't let him get out of it by hitting a soft, high floating return.* Be alert to move forward and volley this shot from the midcourt area so your opponent does not have time to recover. This situation generally occurs when you hit a particularly sharp shot which pulls your opponent wide of the court, out to the end of his reach, and off balance. Because he is in such difficulty, his options are limited. He is likely to miss if he tries a difficult, hard-hit shot. His best play (and yours, if you should be in this position) is to hit the ball back high over the net, aiming deep crosscourt. By high, I mean at least six or seven feet over the net, if not an actual lob. This allows him time to recover a good court position without taking much risk.

If you let your opponent hit this shot, it will be difficult for you to generate enough pace to hurt him on your next shot because his ball will be slow-moving and bounce up high. He will have turned a severely disadvantaged situation into an even one with little cost to himself in terms of risking an error. That's a good deal for him—and one you must deny him whenever possible. You do this by the threat of the volley. If you pick off a few of these high shots with volleys, he will be forced to try to power his way out of trouble and end up making mistakes.

This leads to another general rule: *Never hit a more difficult shot than necessary to accomplish a particular objective.* In the situation in which a player is pulled off the court, his chances of winning the point at that instant are far less than fifty-fifty. If he tries to hit a forcing shot, he may hit an occasional winner, but he is more likely to miss. However, if he can just find a low-risk way to get back to even, he will have made a substantial net gain. The high, floating crosscourt serves that function. Taking *unnecessary* risks costs matches. In that sense, tennis is like poker. You can occasionally win by filling in an inside straight, but you will get very hungry trying to make a living that way. Neither tennis nor poker is a game of chance. In the long run, the high-percentage players win.

This does not mean that you shouldn't take *any* risks. It means you should take only those risks which maximize your probability of winning the point when all factors are taken into account. Consider, for example, the situation in which one player has his opponent off court and has a hefty area clear in which to go for a winner. There are an infinite number of shots which he might try, but they are certainly not all equal in terms of his probability of winning the point. If he hits the ball very hard and very close to the line, his chances of hitting a winner are maximized, but his chances of making an error are also maximized. If he hits it very easy and very far away from the line, his chances of missing the shot are minimized, but his chances of hitting a winner are also minimized. Somewhere between these extremes is his highest percentage shot, taking into account such other factors as how fast his opponent runs and how strong a shot he is likely to hit if he reaches the ball.

This would be a time-consuming calculation for a powerful computer and a sophisticated programmer, yet great tennis players make it with incredible accuracy thousands of times per match in microseconds. The small-percentage difference between the best and a less good calculation does not make a great deal of difference in a single shot or point. But the calculation must be made every time a ball is struck, and after a while those differences start to add up. The cumulative effect of taking bad risks can cause a player with superior power and accuracy to lose to a player with good judgment. It's like gambling in a casino where certain bets give the house an advantage of only 1 percent (your 49.5 percent compared to their 50.5 percent). On a single roll of the dice your chances of winning are nearly even. But over the course of 1,000 rolls, your chances of coming out ahead are virtually nil. That's why in a tennis match, even a small disadvantage in percentages will kill you if you allow it to operate over the thousands of balls being hit.

One way you can slant the percentages in your favor is the judicious use of the net, even if your opponent is clever in his choice of shot. For example, it is a good play to serve and volley often enough to keep your opponent perpetually in doubt as to your intentions. If you don't come to the net behind your serve, he has the freedom to hit high, deep, floating returns off your best serves and to get even in the point with minimal risk of error. The possibility that you may serve and volley forces him to continually hit lower and harder returns than he might like. This, in turn, will cause him to make a few extra errors.

The net attack becomes more likely to succeed as the points become more crucial, particularly at the higher levels of the game. As I mentioned earlier, an assault on the net puts the baseliner under pressure. There is a well-known relationship between performance level and an athlete's degree of excitement or arousal. If the athlete is not aroused at all, his performance is poor. As arousal increases, performance improves until it reaches a peak, after which it starts to fall as arousal continues to go up. This means that you will perform best if you are moderately excited, but will do worse if you are not excited at all *or* too excited.

Pressure, of course, raises an opponent's level of arousal. At an early stage of a match, say 2-all in the first set, the arousal level may be low and attacking the net may excite the baseliner just enough to stimulate some good passing shots. But at 5-all in the third set, when he is under great pressure to begin with, a net attack can raise the baseliner's level of arousal to such uncomfortable heights that hitting a successful passing shot becomes very difficult. Brad Gilbert spent many years working on his net game because of this fact. In college, he was *strictly* a baseliner. (His teammates joked that he came to the net only to check its height or to shake hands.) But on the pro tour he found that passing shots which were routine early in the match became hard to hit in the late stages. Although he makes a living with his passing shots, even Gilbert found himself choking if the points became important enough. So he learned to come to the net himself on the big points so the other guy could choke first.

And there are other ways to gain an advantage in the pressure situations, particularly when your opponent is under more pressure than you are. These are generally times when your opponent is ahead and has a chance to close out a crucial game or point. Most people, for example, feel a lot of pressure when they are serving for the set or match. They are also likely to get tight when they have an advantage point on your serve or sometimes when they have an advantage point on their own serves, especially if it is an important game.

These are all times when your opponent's nerves may cause him to miss easy shots or try something that is tactically foolish. The last thing you want to do in these situations is to let your opponent off the hook by missing quickly yourself. This is where you need to get tough. Play consistent, high-percentage tennis and force your opponent to come up with great shots to beat you.

Another tactical decision point is whether to try to break up your opponent's game by confusing him or to work on grinding him down with a more persistent type of plan. Arthur Ashe and Rod Laver, for example, constantly varied their spins, power, placements, and strategies. Their opponents never knew what they were going to do next. Charlie Pasarell, Arthur Ashe's best friend on the tour and the #1 ranking player in the United States in 1967 (now a big tournament promoter and hotel developer), needled him by claiming that it worked because Arthur didn't know what he was going to do next himself, but Charlie lost the exchange because Arthur said the same thing about him and Arthur had a Wimbledon championship under his belt to give his words weight. In fact, they were both shrewd competitors and their style of play was no picnic for an opponent. Against this type of player you are constantly off balance and get no rhythm. It is very difficult to play well, and you soon find there is literally no ball too easy to miss. On the other hand, the player employing this strategy gets no rhythm or continuity in his own game, so he tends to make extra mistakes too.

The alternative approach was employed by people like Pancho Gonzales, Jack Kramer, and John Newcombe. They were very methodical and persistent in their attacks. They invariably chipped their backhand service returns low, got their first serves in often, hit their first volleys deep, and rarely made mistakes. These champions felt that if they were able to execute their own strategies properly, their opponents wouldn't be able to do much about it. Their opponents pretty much knew what to expect and were able to play their own games normally, but they generally didn't have enough artillery or staying power to withstand the attack. The advantage of using this approach is that you are able to maintain your own rhythm and keep your error rate down. The disadvantage is that your opponent can do the same thing.

Which of these approaches best suits your game depends on your personality and capabilities. The grind-'em-up strategy works best for conservative, persistent types who like to knock heads and don't mind staying at a repetitive task for a while. Using constant variety seems best suited to individuals who are comfortable with risks, bore more easily, and possess a wide assortment of shots. (The former are likely to have the mentalities of accountants or engineers; the latter, real estate developers or commodities traders.) Attempting a strategy which runs counter to your personality (playing against type, as they say in show business) does not usually work.

I, myself, have the proclivities of an engineer. I am averse to risk, persistent, and diligent. But when I played at UCLA, my coach, J. D. Morgan, always insisted that I hit aggressive returns off an opponent's second serve. "Go for it if he misses the first one," J.D. always said. "That's what the 'players' do." And I dutifully followed his advice for years, with just enough success to keep me at it. Eventually, however, a trend became apparent to me. On less important points, I hit the returns well; on big points, when I was nervous, I missed more frequently. My inherent conservativism made me uncomfortable taking big risks in crucial situations. When I forced it, it caused me to miss. I was better off hitting the return solid and low all the time, never missing it, and waiting for my opponent to make mistakes. I simply could not make myself be something I was not, although I tried hard enough. As a young player I was not really aware of what personality type I had, much less that this should have any relationship to my choice of strategy. Later I learned it was a crucial factor.

Personality was the key factor in determining what type of game style was best for John Van Nostrand when he first came to Pepperdine some years ago. John was talented but not highly successful in the juniors. He was big, strong, fast, and played an all-court game. He served well, came to the net some, stayed on the baseline some, and generally oscillated between attack and defense. But John was impatient, emotionally volatile, and prone to nervousness in important situations. This made defense unsuitable for him because it requires its practitioners to spend hours grinding opponents down and to pass them consistently under pressure.

So I had John work on becoming a relentless attacking

player by serving and volleying, coming to the net on opponents' second serves, and attacking the net at every opportunity. John kept the points short and forced his opponents to hit tough passing shots in pressure situations instead of having to hit them himself. This suited him perfectly, and he went on to become an outstanding All-American. Although he certainly had the physical ability to be an excellent baseliner, Van Nostrand's temperament would never have allowed him to pull it off successfully.

So in deciding what type of game you should play, be sure to take into account your particular personality traits in addition to your physical abilities. Analyze your performance on the court; evaluate what makes you feel most (and least) comfortable and confident. Then structure your game around that foundation.

TAMING THE WIND AND ELEMENTS

14

Playing in the wind is a frequent fact of life. Most people feel it is one of life's little burdens. But the player who understands the effects of the wind and other elements and adjusts his game accordingly is actually able to benefit from the situation.

Let me give you an example from my own experience. One swirling, blustery afternoon at Wimbledon in 1965, I faced third-seeded Jan Eric Lundquist, the Swedish champion and Europe's number one player. He was tall, had a huge serve, and had honed his skills on the fast indoor courts of his native land. One week earlier, we had played for the first time on the grass at Queen's Club in London, the historic "warm-up" tournament for Wimbledon, and he had beaten me in two routine sets. Jan Eric was very good indeed when the air was still. But that day conditions were different. The air was *not* still, and I had high hopes for a more profitable result.

I had learned my tennis as a youngster in Tucson, Arizona, a typical windy Southwestern town. In those early days pack rats and dust storms were the area's main attractions, so fast-moving air had been a fact of life for me. I had no choice but to make my peace with it. As I progressed, an understanding of the wind became deeply incorporated into my game. To me, "playing tennis" and "playing tennis in high winds" were the same thing. Walking onto the grass of Wimbledon with Jan Eric that afternoon, I knew the winds gave me a substantial advantage. As Brer Rabbit said to Brer Fox, "Heck, I was born and raised in that briar patch."

We split the first two sets, as the wind nullified some of his previous advantages over me. His powerful first serve, which had punished me with jackhammer consistency at Queen's, was landing all over the place because his high toss was blown repeatedly out of its accustomed orbit. And the pinpoint accuracy that had previously cut my little offense to shreds was also nowhere in sight. His shots were now no more effective than mine, and I was used to playing with shots of dubious effectiveness. It was a shock to his talented system. And I must admit, as I began to get the upper hand in the third set, the standard of tennis was somewhat less than that which customarily brings the Wimbledon audiences to their feet. (Except, possibly, to rush out at intermission and buy refreshments.) I eventually won the third and fourth sets and, as I bounded forward to shake hands—with Jan Eric's laments about "abominable conditions" still ringing in my ears—I was not at all embarrassed to enjoy one of my greatest victories. Sure, if the match had been played under tranquil skies I probably would have lost, but it wasn't. By the same token, if my mother had been Queen Elizabeth I would be the king of England too.

High wind is present during many important tennis matches. It cannot be wished away, unless you have a better relationship with the Almighty than I do, so you must assimilate a new set of tennis concepts. The first and most important is to recognize that both you and your opponent will make more errors than usual. Under these circumstances most people accept with admirable equanimity the additional errors their opponents make, but have somewhat more difficulty with their own. We all have sort of an error thermostat which is triggered when our errors rise above a certain level, no matter what the cause. Even if the match is being played in a hurricane, most people will, irrationally, get irritated if they make more than their usual quota of easy mistakes. The first thing to do in high wind is to reset your thermostat. Accept the additional easy errors unemotionally. Expect them. Irritation is a fast track to disaster.

The old maxim is "Wind is a great equalizer," but in most cases just the opposite is true. The better player has an even greater advantage. Wind favors the clearheaded and mentally strong. It tests the emotional stability of the contestants and it is in just this area that the better players tend to be good. (It is, in fact, often the only reason they are the "better" players.) Hotheads and excuse makers, on the other hand, have a field day blaming the conditions for their problems. Their games fall apart because they become angry instead of accepting conditions as they are. Embracing the inevitable sets the stage for making technical adjustments to the wind.

The first of these adjustments is to shorten the backswing on your ground strokes. This is because the ball will blow off its customary flight path. Trajectory will be more difficult to calculate. By the time the racket has gotten around after a long backswing, the ball is likely to be somewhere other than expected, resulting in a mishit. A short stroke brought forward at the last instant is easier to time.

For the same reasons, your stroke on the volley should also be shortened. Since it is already quite short on hard, low balls you don't have to change anything here. But on high, floating balls it will not profit you to take the longer swing necessary for the immediate kill. You'll only risk more off-center hits and errors. Be content with hitting an extra volley or two before finishing the point.

Since wind reduces the precision of all strokes, it will, in any case, make it difficult to volley with enough accuracy for the quick kill. By the same token, the ground stroker's reduced accuracy makes it difficult to hit passing shots, so a new equation develops between baseliner and volleyer. Both are less effective with their shots, so both must be prepared to run more and hit extra balls. The legs still work fine in the wind, so mobility can be substituted for accuracy. The balance must shift away from shotmaking toward maneuvering.

On the baseline it pays to hit the ball relatively hard even with the wind at your back. (This advice may have more relevance at the higher levels of the game, where the players have the ability to take a short backswing and still hit with power and control.) This is because the quicker the ball reaches its destination, the less time the wind has to act on it. Accuracy is improved because reducing the duration of wind action reduces the deviation of the ball from its intended course.

I must confess that when I say "Hit the ball hard," I am nervous that this will be interpreted as "Just go out and slug the ball." Hitting the ball *too* hard will, of course, cause an unacceptable number of errors. I just mean to hit the ball rather hard, but always stay within the limits of your control.

Many players believe that when the wind is at your back, it is best to hit the ball easier and let the wind carry it. This works to some extent, but not well enough, particularly at higher levels of play. It puts you, to too great an extent, in the hands of the elements rather than your own ability.

When the wind is behind you, additional topspin is helpful to keep the ball in the court. When the wind is against you, a flatter stroke is better to give the ball additional velocity to overcome the retarding action of the wind. (This again applies best for the advanced player, who may have better control of spin. If you are not accustomed to using topspin, a raging windstorm is not the best place to learn.)

With a crosswind, keep in mind that the dimensions of the court are effectively changed. The court is functionally expanded in the direction against the wind (on the upwind side) and reduced in the direction with the wind (on the downwind side). It is as if the whole court had been shifted some distance toward the wind (see Diagram 29).

There is extra room, for example, to hit passing shots along the upwind sideline, but reduced room along the downwind sideline (see Diagram 30).

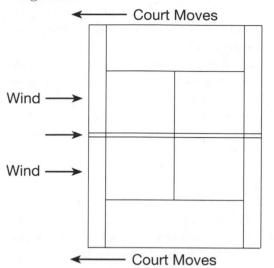

Diagram 29

Court Moves ←

Wind →

→

Wind →

← Court Moves

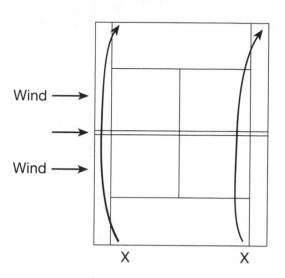

Diagram 30

Wind →

→

Wind →

X   X

When there is no clear opening, therefore, it pays to hit passing shots toward the upwind sideline. Only try to pass toward the downwind side when the volleyer leaves you an extra opening.

In crosscourt rallies on the baseline, the player hitting toward the upwind side has the advantage of safety. An errant wide ball will often be blown back into the court. On the other hand, the player hitting toward the downwind side has the advantage of aggression because well-executed wide shots will be blown farther afield, taking your opponent extra steps out of court. In Diagram 31 player A has the aggression advantage and player B the safety advantage.

So if you are feeling confident and in a mood to gamble, play the downwind side. If you are less secure and want to play conservatively, work the upwind side.

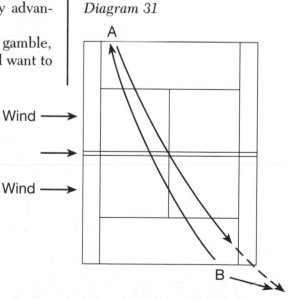

Diagram 31

A

Wind →

→

Wind →

B →

Serving is generally a problem in wind because the ball toss becomes unreliable. You can alter your toss to adjust, but that will help only to a minor extent. Nothing will completely solve the problem. Under these circumstances, do your best to avoid hitting second serves by getting your first serve in. (There are few feelings more disturbing on big points than playing Lotto on second serve. You throw the ball up into the maelstrom, take a swing, and where it will land is a function only of your attendance record at religious services.) Forgo the big, flat first serves and simply spin the ball in. Big serves will tend to miss more than usual anyway because the tolerance is thin to begin with. Everything must be exactly right at the best of times for them to go in, and with wind playing havoc with your toss, everything is hardly likely to be exactly right. The few that go in will not compensate for the double faults.

The wind becomes an enormous factor on the lob. Even a light wind will have a dramatic effect on a lob because the ball moves slowly over a great distance and gives the wind an extraordinarily long time to act. The wind can give a significant advantage to a lobber who really knows what he is doing. The cardinal rules are: (1) Lob offensively *against* the wind and (2) Lob defensively *with* the wind. Trying it the other way around almost invariably leads to disaster. Using the wind properly, however, can turn your lob into a diabolical weapon.

When your opponent comes to the net with the wind at his back, the first shot to think of, if you are not too rushed by his approach, is an offensive lob. You can hit the ball rather hard so that it goes quickly over his head, and the wind will slow the ball so that it drops into the court. A strong wind will give you tremendous leeway on this shot. You can swing away with some abandon and hardly miss.

If the volleyer closes in to his normal position, he will be helpless against this shot. He simply cannot move back quickly enough to cover it. You may be able to catch him again and again until he finally wises up and moves back. An adept lobber, under these conditions, can pin the volleyer back almost to the service line out of respect for the offensive lob. On the other hand, a defensive lob against the wind will tend to land short. If your opponent chooses to let it bounce, the ball will often blow back toward the net, making the put-away very easy. If you decide to hit a defensive lob against the wind, ignore the dictates of your senses and hit it harder and deeper than seems at all reasonable.

But when the wind is at your back, the high, defensive lob really comes into its own. The trajectory should be nearly vertical—the following wind will carry the ball deep in your opponent's court. Timing the overhead will be very difficult and a savvy opponent will usually let the ball bounce. The wind will continue to help after the bounce by blowing the ball back toward the fence. Putting this type of overhead away will not be easy.

On the other hand, hitting an offensive lob with a tailwind should only be attempted by masochists who enjoy seeing their own blood in a fight. It is highly unlikely to work. The low, fast-moving ball will probably get over your opponent's head quickly, but the wind will probably carry it, just as quickly, over the baseline. If you have the time to set up, your best option is a hard passing shot, hit with as much topspin as you can control. The wind-aided ball will be upon the volleyer with uncommon speed. If he reaches the ball, the volley will be difficult. If it eludes him, the topspin will bring the ball down into the court.

The two other elements which most commonly affect play are the sun and the court surface. Both have ramifications which are somewhat obvious, but they must be mentioned because they are so often forgotten during play. Consider the sun. Before the match starts, note its position and remember to offer your net-rushing opponent a liberal dose of lobs when he is on the sunny side. Hitting overheads with a blazing sun in one's eyes requires hardier retinas than most people have. Even the shortest lobs may be unplayable if the sun happens to be in exactly the right spot. So don't forget about the lob, as so many people do, when the sun is at your back and not bothering *you*. The scene on the other side of the net is entirely different and may well be bothering your opponent.

Slippery or fast courts also require adjustments. Both

change the normal balance between offense and defense. Both make offense more profitable. Under these circumstances it pays to take somewhat greater risks with your shots than usual, because your opponent will have greater difficulty reaching the ball. A good shot becomes a very good shot and a very good shot becomes a devastating one.

For example, you might try hitting harder or going down-the-line with your ground strokes more often than usual. On slippery courts, in particular, beat your opponent to the punch and get him skidding around off balance before he gets you skidding around. Once a player is in this type of trouble, it is difficult for him to set up for his shots and hurt you. His lack of accuracy will force him to hit nearer to the center of your court, and you will be able to remain safely on balance and continue jerking him around.

So be aware of how the elements and court conditions affect your play, and use them to take advantage of your opponent.

DOUBLES

15

To play smart doubles, you have to understand the essential differences between singles and doubles. Much doubles strategy is a natural consequence of the fact that each partner of a doubles team is responsible for substantially less territory than in singles. In singles one player has to cover the entire width of the court, which is twenty-seven feet. In doubles there is an additional player but the court is widened by only nine feet, leaving each player responsible for only eighteen feet. The major fallout from this fact is that attacking at the net becomes more profitable in doubles than singles.

The attraction of the net is that balls can be put away more easily than at the baseline. But this is counterbalanced by the risk of being passed. If, for example, singles were played on a court only eighteen feet wide, you would be more inclined to advance to the net because it would be harder for your opponent to pass you. Reducing the passing shot risk obviously shifts the risk-reward equation such that coming to the net is more profitable. (This assumes, of course, that the players have some reasonable ability to volley and hit overheads. If your skill level is such that you feel congratulations are in order if you can just avoid physical injury at the net, these suggestions should be taken with a grain of salt.)

So the first general rule in doubles is the *the team at the net has the advantage*. This rule affects almost all aspects of doubles strategy. Let's start with the serve.

Serving is more of an advantage in doubles than singles because it allows the serving team the first opportunity to advance both players into volley position. This gives them control of the net and a high probability of winning the point. The server's partner should stand approximately halfway between the service line and net and about halfway between the center service line and sideline. In order to hit more damaging volleys it would be advantageous to stand in the center of the court with your nose hanging over the net, but this would be obviously suicidal, since the receiver would have plenty of room to lob or return down-the-line.

Bearing this in mind, the net player should adjust his position depending on the proclivities of the receiver. If you find the receiver never lobs, move in closer to the net. If the receiver never hits down-the-line, move closer to the center of the court to reduce the area into which he dares hit. Some players always position themselves in the same place at the net, no matter what the receivers do. This is a mistake. Be aware of the receiver's capabilities and adjust accordingly.

Without fail, the server should immediately follow his serve forward and join his partner at the net. That establishes the team in a dominating net position with both players forward. This position has a great advantage in doubles, and successful teams establish it whenever possible. The point can then be won with volleys and overheads. Trying to win points by banging winners with your serve is usually a poor-percentage play because too many go awry.

To get to the net, the server need not stop and split step as he would when serving and volleying in singles. In doubles the area of court to be covered by the server is so confined that he knows where the ball is going beforehand. His main problem is to get in fast enough and close enough so that he does not have to hit too many low volleys or volley from behind the service line.

When moving in at high speed, it is important for the server to make a special effort to watch the ball and stay relaxed during the volley. If the return is high and the receiver's partner is at the net, you can sprint forward and hit the first volley at the opponent closest to the net for a winner. If the return is low, the server must play the ball back to the opponent who is farthest away from the net. If both the receiver of the serve and his partner are moving forward, try to volley back soft and low—near the deeper player's feet.

Because your serve offers you the first opportunity to establish your team at the net, the second general rule in doubles is to *get your first serve in*. It is more important to get your first serve in when playing doubles than when playing singles. If the server fails with his first serve, the receiver has an excellent opportunity to attack the second serve and deny the server domination of the net. The receiver can stand in close on the second serve and hit a return so severe that the server dare not follow his delivery to net. Or, from the close-in position, the receiver can move forward behind his return and beat the server to the net.

Even if you have to hit your first serve with less pace than usual to get a high percentage in, it is still advantageous to get the first serve in. Because the receiver will be uncertain as to how hard the serve will be hit, he is forced to stand farther back for his return and will be in a more defensive frame of mind. He is prepared to react rather than attack. This makes him less likely to hit an offensive return or charge to the net behind his return and contest domination of the net with the server.

Where should you serve in doubles? On a strictly geometric basis the best place to serve is down the middle. From this position it is difficult for the receiver to hit down-the-line and pass the partner stationed at the net. It also reduces the angle for the return intended to pass the server who is moving forward. Finally, it enables the server's partner to poach more easily—that is, move across the court at the net in front of the server and intercept the return—because there is less concern with the down-the-line return.

The wide serve is certainly useful in many situations as well. If a player has a weaker side, it may be necessary to serve wide to exploit it. If the receiver rarely returns down-the-line, the wide serve can set up a poach for the partner at the net because the return has to travel a long distance and the receiver is momentarily out of position. It can even be useful without a poach because the receiver can be pulled out of court and the server will have plenty of room in which to volley.

However, the wide serve is generally more risky into the receiver's forehand. This is because the forehand can be hit harder from an off-balance position and more easily slapped down-the-line or sharply crosscourt. The wide serve to the backhand is better because if it is hit one-handed, the receiver will lack strength at the end of his reach, and if it is hit two-handed the receiver will lack reach and will have difficulty getting to the ball.

One of the most effective plays in doubles is the poach. And poaching is a valuable tactic from two standpoints. First, it wins quick points, and second, it damages the opponents psychologically. A receiver who becomes fearful of the net player darting across and tattooing his partner with a volley is a player who is likely to miss a lot of returns. It is hard to watch a fast-moving serve with one eye and a threatening net player with the other. Even if your opponents occasionally pass you down-the-line, it is still advantageous to poach. You will be repaid with interest in missed serve returns and discomfited opponents.

In fact, there is nothing more soothing to a receiving team than to know that the server's partner will not poach. The receiver knows exactly where to hit every time. Instead, make him worry. Move around. Force him to make a split-second decision on each return as to whether to hit crosscourt or down-the-line. He will never get into a comfortable groove.

The two keys to poaching are: (1) timing and (2) making the move itself. Your path on the poach should always be diagonal—across the net *and* forward. Ideally, you want to end up very close to the net so you can volley hard enough to make your opponents ingest the ball. Many players make the mistake of just moving laterally. This works adequately on high volleys (although it is still not advisable), but leads to big trouble on low balls. Since you will be out of position after the poach, you cannot afford to let your opponents get the ball back. You are committed to aggression and half measures are worse than useless, so move quickly and close in for the immediate kill.

The timing of the poach is critical. You must pick the proper instant so that the receiver cannot see you move. You should make up your mind whether or not you are going to poach before your partner serves. Then wait until the last possible second. Very shortly after the serve bounces, the receiver must take his eyes off you and focus on the ball. At that split second, assuming he has been blessed with no more than the normal allotment of two eyes, he cannot see you. Move across instantly as fast as you can.

If you find you are being passed too frequently down-the-line, wait a few milliseconds longer. If you are going across but not able to reach the crosscourt return, leave a few milliseconds sooner. You must ultimately discover a timing which balances the risk of being passed with the risk of not reaching the crosscourt return. But in any case, unless you are just a hopeless volleyer, or you move as if lead weights were attached to both legs, or your opponents return like Don Budge and Rod Laver, do not give up on your poaching and let your opponents get comfortable. One exception: If your opponents both stay on the baseline on serve returns and take away your sitting target at the net, you must poach more sparingly.

How often should you plan to poach? A high-level team thinks about getting in at least one poach each service game. This is a tremendous help to the server. I hear statements from losing doubles players like "My partner lost serve *three* times, while I never lost mine once!" They think their partner's poor play on service was responsible for their defeat. What they may not realize is that their immobility at the net left too much responsibility on their partner's shoulders. When the net person is content to merely guard the alley, the server is forced to cover too much ground against opponents who are likely to return well, knowing they have nothing to fear from the poach.

That's why the partner at the net should always constitute a threat and a nuisance. He must be constantly alert for opportunities to get into the play. Even if one has not planned to poach beforehand, a high or slow-moving return that passes anywhere near the middle of the court should be picked off by the net partner. Your attitude at the net should be aggressive, eager to go after any ball even marginally within reach. Defensive thoughts like "Oh, I hope they don't hit this return down my alley" lead to paralysis. The net player, under these circumstances, will be leaning backward and will have difficulty even guarding the alley. Even if you are not a great volleyer, delude yourself with thoughts like "Let me at the ball. I want to nail any volley that I can get my racket on!" This gets your weight forward and puts you in the proper frame of mind for picking off returns which float near the center of the court. Be an animal. It is intimidating.

Once you have mastered the rudiments of poaching, *when* you use this weapon becomes a guessing game with your opponents. You want to go across when the receiver thinks you won't or when there is so much pressure that your opponent does not have the nerve to hit down your alley. An interesting example of the former is when you have just been burned by a down-the-line serve return. Your opponent expects you to now be suitably respectful and stay put. An immediate poach will often shake things up.

You should think of poaching more frequently on important games such as when you have just broken serve or your partner is serving for the set. These are times when your opponents are intent on breaking back, and your partner can use a little help. A couple of judicious poaches here can break the game apart. Another interesting time to poach is when your opponents have break point. They will rarely have the courage to hit down-the-line at this time.

Poaching can also be an effective way to disconcert an

opponent who is returning exceptionally well. If the returns are being hit with high velocity and accuracy, one's natural tendency is to remain rooted in position. This allows your opponent to stay in the groove all afternoon and make horsemeat out of your partner. Although you will have the consolation of being able to lament losing because your partner could not hold serve, you would be better off taking a few chances and trying to change the situation. A few poaches will at least make your opponent think and may disrupt his timing.

When your team is receiving, you must first decide whether to attack or defend. If you choose to attack, the partner who is not receiving serve should be positioned just inside the service line. Remember, however, that having one player up and one back is a disadvantageous position when facing two people at the net. Its only purpose is to allow the receiver to join his partner at the net as soon as possible or for the partner at the net to poach—in this case, move across in front of his partner and intercept the server's first volley—if the return is good.

Many receiving teams, however, remain one up, one back throughout the point. This allows the serving team the best of all worlds. Once established at the net, they can hit all difficult volleys back to the opponent on the baseline. As soon as they get an easy one, they can blast it at the opposing net player, who stands around through most of the point adding no value but making quite a convenient target. He might as well have a bull's-eye on his chest. At close range a sharp volley or overhead at him will usually end the point in a hurry.

If the receivers choose to defend, it's best to position both partners on the baseline. This denies the serving team any target. They will have to hit through two entrenched defenders. When you are defending in this position and in doubt of where to hit, aim down the middle over the low part of the net. This is a low-risk shot and leaves the volleying team with no angle from which to hit a winning volley. It also pulls both net players toward the center of their court and opens up holes along the sidelines for your next ground stroke.

When defending, you should also make liberal use of the lob. Hit these as high as possible or, if the volleyers have moved in close to the net after having faced several ground strokes, you can hit an offensive lob with a low trajectory and higher velocity. If the offensive lob gets over the volleyers' heads, the defenders should immediately go on offense and both rush to the net. Now you have the advantage in the point and your opponents must defend.

Another tactic to use when your team is receiving is to aim a few crisp returns down-the-line at or past the net person. Do not overhit and miss these. They must go in the court to achieve the desired effect. Do this at the beginning of the match and it proclaims immediately that you are willing and able to return down-the-line, that you do not have undue respect for the net person, and that anyone contemplating poaching had better beware. This will pay dividends later in the match by making your opponents reluctant to poach on important points.

And to not overlook this return during the body of the match as well. A solid, low return directly at the net person is difficult to volley. The net person is stationary and cold. It is easier for the server to volley because he is moving and prepared to hit the shot. Thus, the surprise down-the-line can produce a cheap error or, at the minimum, keep the net person rooted in position. And if the second serve is weak and short, the down-the-line return can be a point winner. It may, in fact, be the easiest shot you get at the net player.

Another important rule in doubles is to *avoid getting caught in no-man's land,* between the service line and baseline. Whether you are serving or receiving, move forward decisively and quickly whenever you opt to advance to the net. If you get caught between the service line and baseline you are vulnerable, just as you are at net. But in no-man's land, unlike at the net, your vulnerability is not counterbalanced by an ability to attack your opponents. You can be hurt, but cannot hurt anybody yourself—the worst of all situations.

So when you decide to serve and volley or follow your return to the net, make sure you move fast enough to get inside the service line. You must make a conscious commitment beforehand to get in quickly. Half measures or look-and-decide-later techniques will get you caught too deep in the court.

Now, if your team is serving, where should you hit your volleys? Normally, aim the first one down the middle of the court as deep as possible. Attempting an angle on the first volley is difficult because the server is not yet close enough to the net to have the wide angles open. If you try to hit an angle, it is unlikely to be severe enough to cause the defenders great difficulty. But on the negative side of the ledger, it will create openings along a sideline through which the defenders can hit drives. If both defenders are on the baseline, you should also direct subsequent volleys down the middle and deep unless there is an obvious opening. Hitting down the middle pulls both defenders to the center of their court and produces openings in the areas they have been forced to abandon. If the receivers leave a man at the net and one on the baseline, work the ball as suggested earlier—hit tough volleys back deep to the baseliner and easy ones at the net person.

If all four players are at the net, the team that gets closest to the net soonest will usually win the point. If you must hit a low volley, hit it back soft and low and move forward quickly. If you get a high volley, charge in and try to get on top of the net. Then smack it at or between your opponents. The key in these exchanges is to be mobile *forward*. No matter where your opponents are, in fact, if the ball is high or slow, move forward as far and as fast as you can. Many players make the mistake of standing still on high volleys and taking a long swing at the ball. If you have any time at all, get your legs going forward. Only from close in can you consistently put the ball away.

When opposing players face each other at close range at the net, physical intimidation can become a factor. I received a graphic lesson facing Chuck McKinley, the 1963 Wimbledon singles champion, in a doubles match in Tucson in 1964. I had, by some miracle, beaten Chuck in the singles semifinal earlier in the day, and he was looking for blood in the doubles—mine. Chuck was built like a little tank—short, stocky, and with incredibly strong wrists. He could smack balls from any position with shuddering force. (And when the urge took him, he was capable of performing original research on just how deeply a tennis ball could penetrate human tissue.)

Chuck returned serve from the backhand side in doubles, and one of his favorite plays was to chip the return soft and low and charge in behind it like an enraged bull. His acceleration was so prodigious that he could get within a few feet of the net by the time the server hit his first volley. And God help the server's partner if that volley was high. Chuck liked to take those on the dead run and aim full-swing volleys at the net man's midsection.

I found myself at the net on one such point as Chuck hit a particularly squirrely little backhand chip off my partner's serve and roared in at warp speed. (As the ball settled down around my partner's ankles I developed a powerful urge to cross myself, even though I am Jewish.) Seeing Chuck barreling in so fast panicked my partner, and he threw up a desperation lob volley. Oh-oh, it was short. And of all the fearsome shots in Chuck's repertoire, his overhead was the most fearsome. I had as much chance of dodging that ball as I did of becoming chancellor of Austria. For weeks afterward I wore, on my abdomen, a black and blue mark the size and shape of a tennis ball, so clearly imprinted that if I really looked closely I was sure I could make out the name *Wilson* on it.

The effect on my psyche was dramatic. From that moment forward my plans for winning the match magically metamorphosed into plans for leaving the court alive. I was scared, paralyzed, and, needless to say, completely ineffective.

I am not suggesting you spend doubles matches deliberately trying to hit your opponents. That is unsportsmanlike and leads to unpleasant, antagonistic matches. But some gentle intimidation, legitimately and subtly introduced, can certainly become a factor. If you get an overhead or high volley with your opponents at the net, you might put a little extra weight into the shot as you hit it between them or near their feet. This ensures that the ball will not come back, and the extra force in the shot makes a subconscious impression on your opponents. They might even flinch next time, lest a slight misdirection on your part send the ball somewhere where they could get hurt. They will just be a little less likely to stand in there and reflex your shot back.

Chuck McKinley was, by the way, a great sportsman, and his method of intimidation was not usually as direct and personal as it was in our doubles match. He was just a flamboyant, swing-from-the-floor kind of character, who moved fast and hit hard. Even though he might not be specifically aiming at you, balls were traveling at rather high velocity, and accidents do happen. Anyone playing against him did have to think about it.

If the object in smart doubles is to take over the net, why do so many teams at the recreational level play with both teams having one player at the net and one on the baseline? Although this may seem contradictory to my previous analysis, under certain circumstances this formation has some charm to it. The key here is that *both* teams have one person up and one back. It allows the net person to volley any shot within reach and the baseliner to cover everything else. The point will usually develop with the baseliners hitting most of the balls and the net people watching. It will often end when an errant ground stroke drifts within reach of a volleyer and he smacks it at the opposing volleyer.

When your team is in this situation, remember that if you can get both players on your team to the net and your opponents remain one up, one back, you have a decided advantage. If you are on the baseline, try to join your partner at the net as soon as possible. A good way to do this is to hit a lob over your opponents' net player and follow it in. Otherwise, hit as deep as possible in order to elicit a short reply and use this as an avenue to the net. If, however, you are unable or unwilling to get to the net, your partner who is already at the net should look for the first opportunity to poach—move across the center and hit the volley at the opposing net player. This will usually suffice to end the point.

When your opponents are returning serve well and you

are having difficulty holding serve in the normal formation, try changing to the Australian formation. Here the server stands immediately adjacent to the center line and his partner lines up at the net in front of him on the same side of the center line. When serving to the forehand court, for example, the server stands just to the right of the center line and his partner also stands to the right of the center (see Diagram 32).

The server should usually aim the delivery down the middle and follow it in as shown in Diagram 32.

Diagram 32

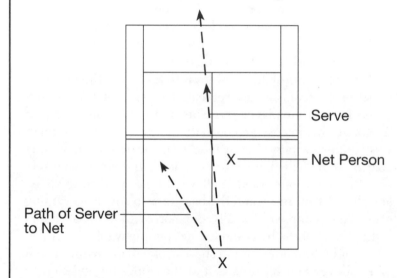

Serve

X——— Net Person

Path of Server to Net

X

With this formation the server is responsible for the left side of the court and the net person for the right. In the normal formation the server would cover the right side and the net person the left. The receiver must now return down-the-line to avoid the net man rather than hitting the normal crosscourt return.

Why don't people always use the Australian formation? Why isn't it the "normal" formation? Because it is geometrically disadvantageous relative to the conventional formation. The receiver can hit the ball past the net-rushing server more easily in the Australian formation, particularly if the serve is hit wide. This is because a return traveling down-the-line (as it does in the Australian formation) goes a shorter distance before passing the oncoming server than a return traveling crosscourt (as it does in the normal formation).

In Diagram 33 the ball will have passed the server when it reaches the shaded area behind the service line. Note the distance down-the-line, A, is shorter than the distance crosscourt, B.

With the Australian formation, it is therefore slightly more difficult for the server to cover court on his first volley. On the other hand, it may be worth the price in order to disconcert the receiver, who is now forced to change the

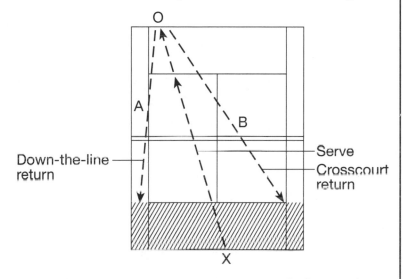

Diagram 33

Down-the-line return

Serve

Crosscourt return

direction of the return away from one which may have grown comfortable.

In summary, here are a few general rules to keep in mind for sound doubles play:

1. The team at the net has the advantage.
2. Get a high percentage of first serves in play.
3. Try to establish both partners at the net together; otherwise both should stay on the baseline.
4. Avoid getting caught between the service line and baseline.
5. Play difficult shots to the opposing player farthest from the net, aiming for his feet whenever possible.
6. When in doubt, hit down the middle of the court.
7. Move forward during volley exchanges.

INDEX